I0481597

WORD for the Wise:

Using Microsoft Office Word

for

Creative Writing

and

Self-Publishing

Jaye W Manus

This book is dedicated to all my wonderful clients whose countless Word docs forced me to learn how to use Word.

Introduction

Part I: What To Do Before You Write

Part II: What To Do While You Write

Part III: What To Do After the Writing is Done

Part IV: What To Do When the Writing and Editing are Done but Before Formatting

Part V: Formatting Word Docs for Specific Purposes

Introduction

I'll tell you first off, I'm no Microsoft Office Word expert.

What I am is an expert in using Word *as a writer*.

I've been using computers since the 1980s and have used a variety of word processors (which I used like fancy typewriters sans Wite-Out and carbon paper). When I purchased my first Windows PC the Microsoft Office Suite came pre-installed, so I used Word, because it was there, to produce manuscripts I then printed, stuck in a box, and mailed to either my agent or editor.

That changed in 2011 when self-publishing became a viable means of connecting writers and readers and I decided to try my hand at formatting ebooks. At first, it was just for fun. The more I learned, the more I wanted to learn, and it didn't take long before people were asking me to format their ebooks and I was in business.

That's when it dawned: For all those years I'd been using Word wrong. Not only wrong, but *destructively*, making a whole lot of extra work for myself and damaging files.

Word is an excellent word processor, one of the most powerful on the market. All that power comes with a price: Where the act of composing fiction or nonfiction is a simple process (in technical terms) Word is complicated. It's right there in the name itself: Microsoft *Office* Word. It's a *productivity* program for businesses; not a *publishing* program for writers of commercial fiction and nonfiction.

For writing a report or a business proposal or a policy & procedures manual, it's one of the best programs around. For writers, though? It's kind of like driving a Porsche Carrera to the grocery store.

Even so, just about every writer I deal with uses Word. Even Mac users. Even writers who wouldn't touch a Microsoft program send material that has been exported as a Word doc. Word is everywhere thanks to Microsoft having installed it on all Windows PCs for decades. (They no longer give away the Microsoft Office Suite; Word must now be licensed via subscription.)

Smashwords, the largest and heartiest of the aggregators for self-publishers to distribute and sell ebooks, converts Word docs into a wide variety of ebook platforms. (A publisher can also upload an EPUB file to Smashwords.) Other sites now allow self-publishers to upload Word docs. Even Amazon allows it. The conversion processes they use are programmed to recognize and modify the HTML coding in a Word doc.

Writers are using Word to compose their work, and some use it to format ebooks, and others use it to format print-on-demand editions. Even some professional ebook and print formatters use Word. Word might not be the best word processor for writers, but it is everywhere and it's not going away for a long, long time.

I have processed thousands of Word docs, millions and millions of words, from hundreds of clients. The majority of those writers are like me from ten years ago, using the program inefficiently and often destructively. Cleaning up those files is how I've become an expert.

I can help you use Word like an expert, too.

My goals with this book are:

- Teach writers to customize Word to suit their particular needs.
- Teach writers to use the features that actually make their writing lives easier.
- Help writers increase their creative productivity by eliminating destructive practices.
- Teach writers to create the various types of docs used for editorial tasks, digital submissions, ebooks and print-on-demand interior files.

Even if you don't use Word, you might find this book useful. There are dozens of word processors and programs created specifically for creative writing. The majority use the same underlying principles as Word.

I give you my promise. There are no gotchas in this book. No traps. No need for special skills or technical knowledge. I won't use tech-speak because I don't know any; I'm talking to you writer to writer. You don't even need a spectacular memory since many of the things I recommend will require your attention just once. Set it and forget it and write on.

You only need two things to get the most out of this book: a desire to use Word productively and a mouse to click with.

So let's get started.

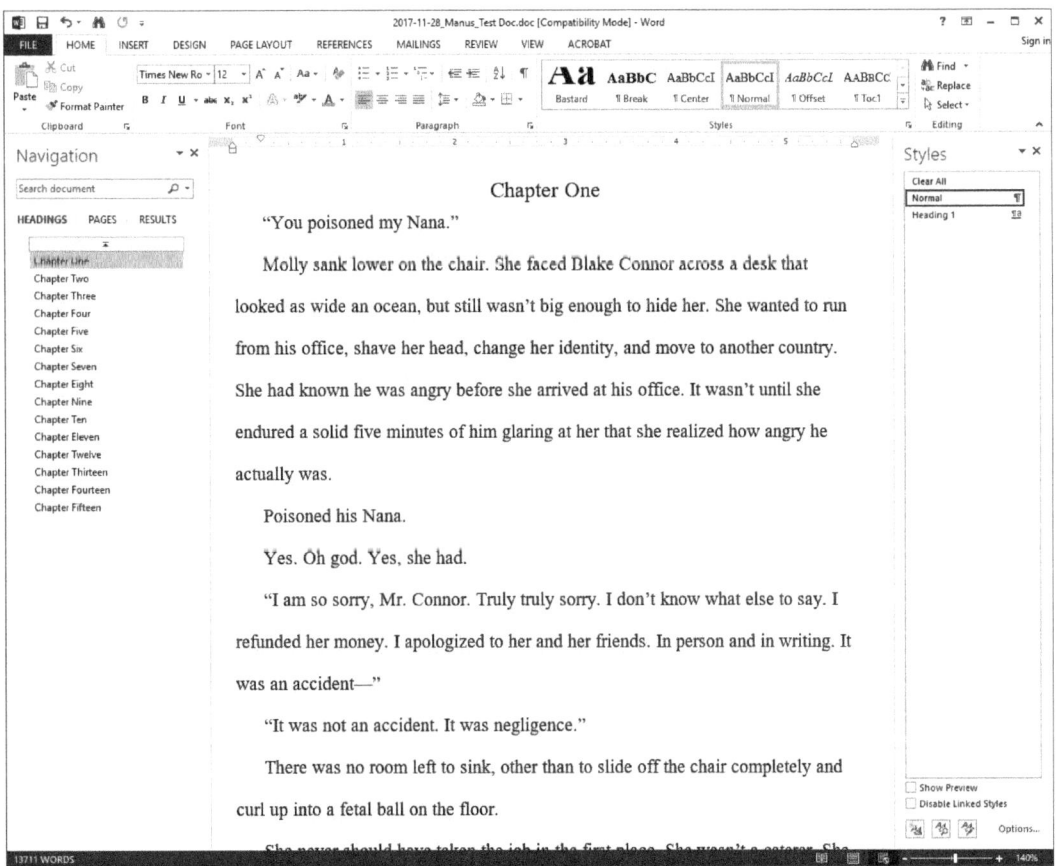

Microsoft Office Word set up for writing fiction.

1: Writing in the Digital Age

If you intend to use MS Word for writing and editing only, it doesn't make much difference which version you use. It's essentially a high-powered type-writer.

If, however, your intent is to use the program to format ebooks and print-on-demand editions, I *highly* recommend you obtain the latest version. Even as Word gets more complicated and feature-laden, it is getting more user-friendly, too. The cost of the program is offset by the time you will save.

The instructions in this book specifically apply to Word 2016. The underlying principles, however, apply to *all* versions of Word, even the earliest versions. The basics of the program—File, Home, Page Layout, Review, etc.—haven't changed too much over the years.

How is it possible to use Word *destructively*? It's not because we—writers—are stupid or technically inept. (Some of us *are* technically inept, but it's not as if we—*cough* *I*—don't have other things going for us.) All you have to do is open a blank doc and start typing. Right?

If all we were doing was creating printed manuscripts in order to mail them to someone, there'd be no point in writing or reading this book.

We're not creating manuscripts; we're creating digital documents that may or may not be printed. To create those digital documents, Word uses HTML coding. A lot of it.

Digital docs are shared. In the case of self-publishers, they are formatted for emails, ebooks and print-on-demand editions. Much of Word's HTML coding, programmed to complement the entire Office Suite of programs and facilitate the creation of business paperwork, turns destructive when the docs are shared or used for purposes other than for what they are intended to do.

There are destructive practices that not only damage Word docs, but reduce creativity and waste time. (I despair a little whenever I receive a heavily "formatted" doc because I know the writer spent a lot of time and energy making everything look just right and the first thing I do is strip out every bit of that formatting.)

Many destructive practices are habits and/or holdovers from the days of print-only files. Others are caused by Word itself—the program makes it very easy, with a few mouse clicks, to turn a simple doc into a gnarly, damaged mess.

What follows are some new ways of thinking that'll make writing and book production easier and less frustrating, while also reducing mistakes and away-from-writing time.

What You See Is *Not* What You Get

If you are creating docs to print at home, with your own printer, then what you see on the screen is pretty much what you'll get.

If you're sharing digital docs, the opposite is true. By sharing I mean formatting it for an ebook or a print-on-demand edition; or sending it in the body of an email or as an attachment. Word not only doesn't play nice with other programs, sometimes it doesn't play nice with itself. That doc you labored over for hours and hours so it'll look gorgeous can turn into an unreadable mess when someone on another computer and/or with another program opens it.

Your safest bet is to assume that what *you* see is not necessarily what anyone who is *not looking over your shoulder* will see.

The easiest way to shift this mindset is to work in Web Layout view.

Go to View> Views and click "Web Layout".

The screen will change so there are no margins or pages. (Word will still display word count.) The beauty of this is that you can adjust the size of the window on the screen—just like viewing a website. No distracting "pages", or obsessing about widows/orphans, or where text breaks on a line, or needing an oversized font in order to work without eyestrain.

To zoom in, either:

a) Go to View> Zoom and click "Zoom" which opens a task menu where you can set page view size;

Or

b) Use the zoom bar at the bottom right of the main screen. Sliding it back and forth changes the page view size.

Tabs and the Space Bar

The Tab key is a relic. Writers depended heavily on it when typewriters ruled, but in the digital age the tab key's only real function is to bounce rapidly from form field to form field.

The major problem with the tab key is that many programs do not recognize Word's tab command or, worse, misinterpret it. In an ebook, tabs can cause unwanted paragraph jumps or line breaks.

In a later chapter I will show you how to set up a doc so you rarely have to use the tab key again—except to bounce from form field to form field. If it's a habit, it's time to break it. Stick a piece of colored paper on the tab key as a reminder to not use it.

The same thing goes for holding down the Space Bar in order to align text on a page. All those spaces are the Devil's Playground when it comes time to share or format your doc. I'll show you in Chapter 3: Set Up Styles how to align text without using the space bar.

If you were taught to insert two spaces between each sentence in a paragraph, unlearn it. The habit won't damage your doc, but it does create one more thing to clean up before the doc can be formatted.

White Space and Blank Lines

One of the biggest wastes of time is using multiple hard returns (Enter) to drop text in order to start a new chapter or section; and using multiple returns to drop chapter heads to the middle of the page; and using multiple returns to indicate scene or section breaks; and using hard returns (Enter) or soft returns (Shift+Enter) to control widows and orphans or the width of a line.

I used to do all that stuff myself. I remember all too well the dismay when a revision in one chapter messed up the pagination and created *new* widows and orphans to deal with.

White space is confusing, too, in a digital document. Digital docs don't have pages. Without a sheet of paper in hand, how is the reader supposed to know if blank lines are deliberate or a mistake?

When I'm writing my rule is: *No blank lines.*

Make this your rule, too, and you'll greatly reduce formatting errors and misinterpretation. In Chapter 5: "Formatting" on the Fly I'll show you how to create docs without any confusing blank lines or white space.

One Size Fits All

There are some who think: *I have this powerful program at my disposal so as long as I format while I write, I'll save time and energy. When I'm done, I'll just save a Word .doc or .docx for the ebook and export a PDF for the print file, and* Ta da! *all done.*

Nuh uh, nope, no way.

Possibly, there are some writers who have day jobs working in big offices and they've taken all the classes and they can understand the tech-speak in manuals and their office has Microsoft Office experts who can answer questions. It is possible they have the skills to make Word behave well enough so that one file can be converted seamlessly into a multitude of formats and platforms.

Possible, but not likely.

Actually, now that I think about it, being an expert in MS Office probably causes its own set of problems for writers since so much of what Word can do is incompatible with commercial writing and self-publishing.

What ends up happening with one-size-fits-all formatting is that it creates monster messes that you can't see or realize are there until files won't convert; or reader complaints come rolling in; or you're getting nasty-grams that tell you to fix the ebook or risk having your book delisted. Not to mention making a lot of extra work that detracts from the creative process; not to mention having to depend on your memory to recall if your chapter heads are 14pt bold or are they 16pt and italicized? Or maybe you forget to insert a chapter heading at all.

When I write, I don't format. In a creative heat, my concern is kicking my characters in the teeth—not worrying about what my chapter headings look like. When it comes time to share or format the file, that's when I concern myself with appearances.

It might seem counter-intuitive, but separating the creative process from the production process does save time. It reduces mistakes and formatting errors. It reduces frustration, too. When a doc is junked up and damaged by over-formatting or inappropriate formatting, it must be repaired. It's easier to not create problems in the first place.

Whether you're outsourcing formatting or doing it yourself, keep your creative process separate from production and just write. I'll show you how to easily produce a Master Doc that makes quick work of formatting a variety of docs for specific purposes.

Save and Save As

Ever had the power go out while you're working? Had a program crash? A hard drive fail? A computer give up the ghost and die?

I'm holding up both hands and waving wildly.

Go to File> Options> Save and check the boxes for "Save AutoRecover every 10 minutes" and "Keep the last autosaved version if I close without saving".

That simple step will prevent much heartache in case of a power outage or other glitch.

I'm a bear about saving my work. Every creative person should be, too.

Not only do I save compulsively while working, I back up my work in the cloud and also on portable storage devices. You can use flash drives, thumb drives, SD and microSD cards, and external hard drives. Digital storage is cheap, and it's the most valuable investment you can make.

In my opinion, one of the most underused Word features is Save As.

Modern computers have tons of storage space—far more than any writer can ever possibly run out of. If, like me, you've been around a while and once used computers with ridiculously tiny RAM while using multiple floppy disks to save your work, you might have to do mental battle against a stingy-storage mind set. Trust me, if you need 5 or 10 or 50 versions of a work in progress your computer has more than enough capability to hold them all.

Keep your files organized in Document folders (rather than on the desktop) and in the file names state their purpose: "First Draft", "Final Draft", "Edit",

"Ebook", "Proofread", and so on and so forth. That makes it easy to search for a file if it is misplaced on the computer or in storage systems.

My process is to write in drafts. The first draft is my rough, often little more than a synopsis or outline. Once I reach the end, I save the file, then do a Save As to create a copy for the second draft. If at the end of that I decide a third draft is warranted, Save As to create a new copy. This retains earlier versions and I don't suffer the regret of losing something to cutting that I didn't really want to cut after I've given it some thought.

Do the same thing with editing and production. Save As creates a doc for editing and another for proofreading. One for ebook formatting and another for a print-on-demand edition and another for an Advance Reading Copy.

Use Save As to make copies, lots of them. Your future self will thank you.

PART I:

What To Do Before You Write

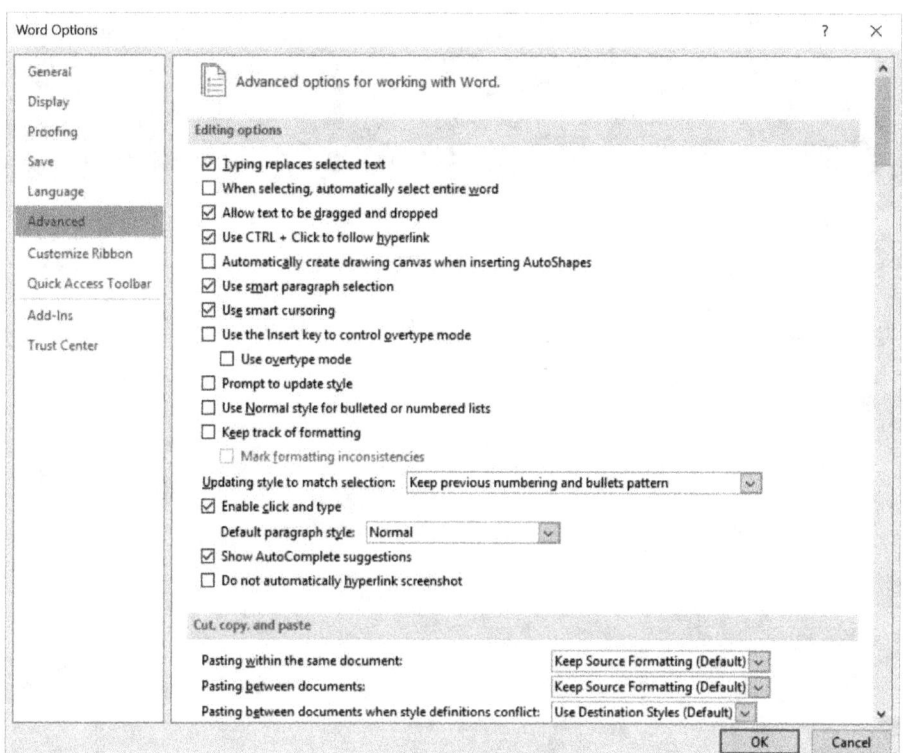

File>Options

Easily turn options on and off to customize Word.

2: Customize Word for Your Working Style

Word is a wonderfully helpful program—if you're working for a corporation, in a big office, and you're *not* a writer, especially a fiction writer. It has auto-correct and auto-format features that make it very easy for Assistant A to type up a memo that looks exactly like the memo typed by Associate B in order to compose a P&L report for Vice President C.

Those same features can be very tempting for creative writers. A mouse click here, a mouse click there, and before you know it your short story or novel is trapped inside a bloated, unmanageable doc that even your mother won't want to (or can't) read. Even worse than that, the multiple Ribbon toolbars and task menus can be intimidating or confusing—a writer fears that touching anything is going to ruin his work.

The cure for this is to set up Word to suit your particular working style.

To customize Word, go to File> Options.

Do not be intimidated by the options and menus. Changing options is as easy as clicking the mouse a few times. You aren't going to wreck anything or damage your files. If you choose an option that you end up disliking or if you find it distracting, change it. (For easy reference, Appendix B contains a list of functions and tasks in File> Options.)

Open Word while you are reading this. Make a copy of your current work in progress and call it Dummy File. Try out options and see what happens.

General

This determines how Word handles files. I leave most of the options turned On. Personalizing Word with your name is essential if you're sharing work for editorial purposes. That way you'll know who makes what change or comment.

Display

I suggest leaving on the default Page display options. "Show document tool/ tips on hover" is especially useful if you have a tendency to forget what an icon means (the way I do).

Turn off everything listed under "Always show these formatting marks on the screen".

(When you're formatting a doc and need to see the marks, go to Home> Paragraph. Click the Show/Hide icon: ¶)

Choose the printing options you need.

Proofing

This one: "Change how Word corrects and formats your text."

Nope, prefer to do that myself, thank you very much.

Do you hate red or green squiggles? Here's where to turn them off. Need the reminders? Turn them on.

Customize spell check and add dictionaries if you have them.

Click the "AutoCorrect Options..." box and it will open the AutoCorrect and AutoFormat menus.

Customize AutoCorrect and AutoFormat to suit your needs and comfort level. You know your own habits and quirks better than anyone else and you know which options are helpful and which are distracting. If you clear everything, Word will act like a typewriter. Choose only those options that enhance your creative process and make your life easier.

My recommendation in AutoFormat> Replace is to activate the "smart quotes" option. Straight quotes have few purposes in fiction or nonfiction. In a commercial product (ebook or print) they look ugly and unprofessional.

Another useful AutoFormat> Replace feature is "Hyphens (--) with dash (—)". That way when you type -- Word will automatically replace it with an em dash.

Tip: Many AutoCorrect and AutoFormat shortcuts can also be accessed in Insert> Symbols> Symbol> AutoCorrect *or* Shortcut Key. That's the quick way to turn features on and off for specific purposes.

Save

Set the AutoRecover option if you haven't already.

In the "Preserve fidelity when sharing the document" menu are the options for embedding fonts. Click on all the options. It will ensure that your editor or beta reader or formatter or printer will see the fonts you used.

Language

These are the options for choosing a language in which to write. Set your language and forget it. English is the default, so if you're writing in English, you can pretty much ignore this menu. If you're writing in another language, this is the place to install the appropriate languages and keyboard features.

> Caution: If you're writing in English, but your story contains a lot of foreign words, *do not* use this menu to install other languages or change your keyboard functionality.

Advanced

This menu is filled with far more options than you'll ever need. (Even if you're using Word to create print documents, chances are you'll only ever use about 2% of the program's features. *Office*, remember?) Under the "Editing" and "Cut, copy, and paste" sub-menus are some handy features to control your cursor and such. Check only those boxes that suit your working style and clear the rest.

Customize Ribbon

I like everything handy so I activate the Ribbon Toolbar with the default settings (shows everything). If you're the easily distracted type turn off the Ribbon display, leaving you with a blank "page" on which to work.

Note: If you prefer viewing the Ribbon toolbar some of the time, but other times you want it to go away, at the far right bottom of the Ribbon there is an up arrow. Click it and the Ribbon collapses, leaving only the Quick Access Toolbar. To restore the Ribbon, click any of the main Ribbon headings and when the full Ribbon appears click the pin icon in the far right bottom.

While we're on the subject, take a look at the Ribbon Toolbar. You'll notice that next to many of the icons are arrows. Clicking those open either options or task menus. Hovering the cursor over an icon will tell you what an icon's function is. In many of the task boxes are arrows in the lower right corners. Clicking those will open panes or task menus. For easy reference, Appendix C: Where do I Find . . . ? contains a list of specific tasks and options in the different Ribbons.

Quick Access Toolbar

This menu allows you to further streamline the appearance of Word. The toolbar displays shortcuts and tools as icons at the top left of the window. Useful if you'd prefer to work without the full Ribbon showing.

Add-ins

This menu displays additional programs such as a PDF maker or OneNote. You can customize some of your add-ins here. If you don't have add-ins or don't know what add-ins are and have never thought about them before, you can leave this menu completely alone and never have to think about it.

Trust Center

This is the security menu. You can change the settings, but it's not recommended that you do.

Customizing Word to suit your particular writing style and creative process is easy and flexible. You know how *you* work and what makes you feel comfortable and creative. You also know what distracts you. Don't be afraid to try out features, turning them on and off until you find the perfect fit for your creative style. If a feature bugs you, turn it off. If you're repeating a particular command, turn on the display or shortcut for it. Make Word work for *you*.

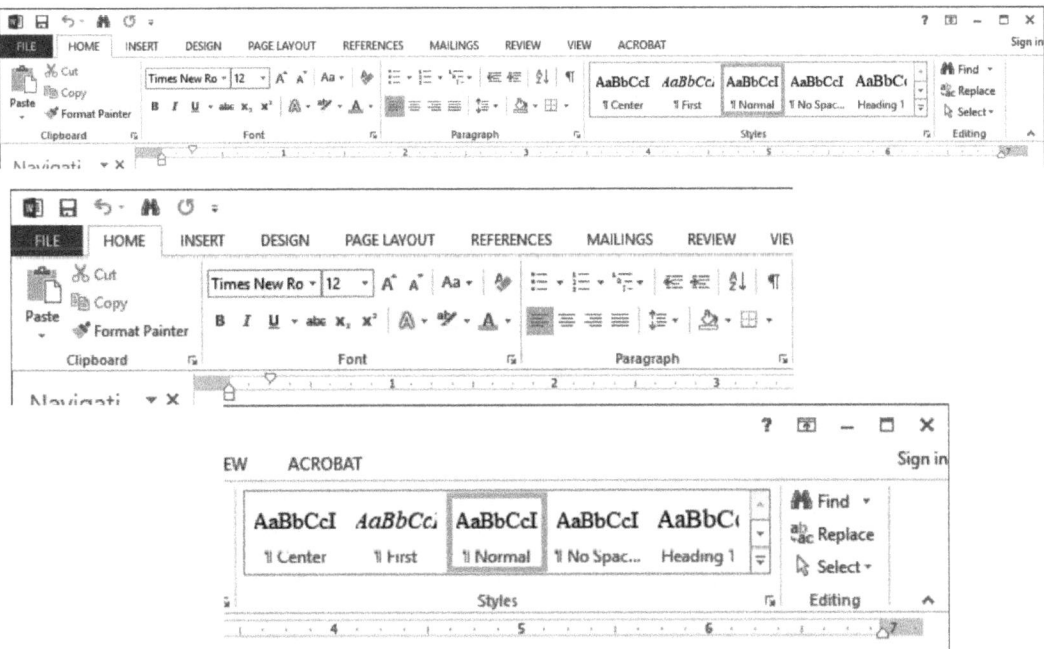

The up-pointing arrow in the lower right corner of the toolbar collapses the Ribbon. Clicking the pin icon that is displayed when the Ribbon is collapsed will restore the full Ribbon.

The arrows in the lower right corners of option boxes open panes or task menus.

Arrows next to or beneath icons open dropdown menus.

3: Set Up Styles

Remember how I told you all word processors work the same? Styles are the reason why. If you get in the habit of using styles, you can use any word processor (or publishing program) as efficiently as you're about to learn how to use Word.

Styles are paragraph and character formatting options for indents, line spacing, fonts, etc.

Word comes preloaded with a wide variety of Document Templates with the styles preset. Just fill in the blanks. Those templates, however, aren't much use for writers. The same goes for the preloaded Styles. They are geared toward office production or home publishers creating invitations or résumés. (I don't think I've *ever* used any of Word's pre-made styles without significant modification.) Any pre-made style can be modified, and custom styles are easy to create.

Formatting ebooks or print-on-demand editions requires a wide variety of styles. *Writing* a novel or short story or essay or article requires only two. Normal and Heading 1.

(Nonfiction might require multiple Heading styles.)

By using those two styles I guarantee that: a) your doc will contain minimal junk and damaging code; b) the first paragraph of your piece will be set up and styled exactly like the final paragraph when you type "The End", even if days, weeks, months or years have passed since you typed "Chapter One".

While you are reading this, open a blank document. Follow along.

Normal

Normal is a body text style. It'll be your default style so that whatever you write will be styled in Normal *until* you apply a different style. Here's how to set it up for creative writing:

Go to Home> Styles and click the open arrow in lower right corner of the styles box. A Styles pane will open. Hover the cursor over Normal and right click. Select "Modify".

A task menu will open.

At the bottom click on "Add to the Styles gallery" and "New documents based on this template".

Next, click Format and from the dropdown menu select Paragraph.

Indents and Spacing
   Alignment: Left
   Outline level: Body Text
   Indentation Left: 0 (zero)
   Indentation Right: 0 (zero)
   Special: First line
   By: 0.25″ (if you prefer narrow indents); 0.5″ (if you prefer deep indents)
   Spacing Before: 0 pt
   Spacing After: 0 pt
   Line spacing: Single (or) 1.5 lines (or) Double
   At: (leave blank)
Line and Page Breaks
   Clear all boxes.
   Click OK.

Next, click Format and from the dropdown menu select Font.

Font
   Font: Times New Roman (or) Courier/Courier New (or) Arial
   Font Style: Regular
   Size: 12pt
   Click OK.
In the main task menu click OK.

From this point forward every new document you open in Word will be styled in Normal. Try it now. Type a few paragraphs. Without using the tab key or the space bar all the paragraph indents are the same. Whether the doc is fifty words or a hundred and fifty thousand, every paragraph will look the same—until you apply a different style.

Access styles from the Home Ribbon Toolbar, or, click the arrow in the corner to open the styles pane. Hover the cursor over any style and right-click, select Modify to open task menus.

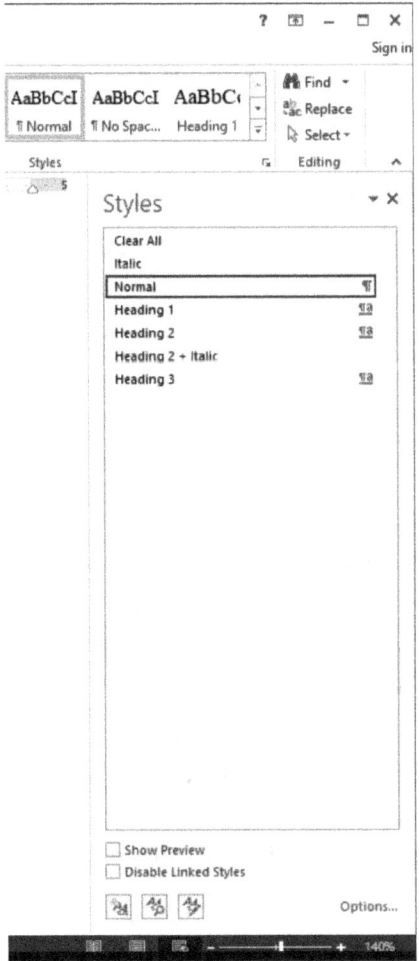

Select Options... to customize the Styles Pane.
Click the icon in the lower left to create a new style.

Some of you might be curling your lips at the font choices. There is a method to the madness. There is no such thing as a universal font. No operating system, be it Windows or OS or iOS or Android, comes pre-installed with every font in existence. Every program has a different way of using and displaying fonts. When docs are shared the recipient's program may or may not contain the font the sender used. In that case, the program will substitute its own font. If the program cannot read the font the recipient will see pink boxes or question marks or bizarre characters. Times New Roman, Courier/Courier New, and Arial are *common* fonts, installed on almost every computer and on many devices, and they're as close to universal as we're going to get. By using them you can safely assume that no matter how the doc is shared, another program or another computer will be able to read what you wrote.

So, if you prefer a serif font, use Times New Roman; if a monofont makes you comfortable, choose Courier/Courier New; if your preference is for sans serif, use Arial.

Heading 1

This style is for chapter/section headers. The best reason to use it during creative writing is that it automatically creates a navigation guide. Plus, it eliminates the need for page breaks. When it comes time to format a doc for a specific purpose the Heading styles make creating tables of contents easy.

Here's how to set it up for creative writing:

Select the text for a heading, such as Chapter One. Go to Home> Styles and click the open arrow in the lower right corner of the styles box to open the Styles pane. Click Heading 1 (a built-in style) to apply it to the selected text. Hover the cursor over Heading 1 and right click. Select "Modify".

The task menu will open.

At the bottom click on "Add to the Styles gallery" and "New documents based on this template".

Next, click Format and from the dropdown menu select Paragraph.

Indents and Spacing
Alignment: Left (*or*) Centered
Outline level: Level 1
Indentation Left: 0 (zero)

Indentation Right: 0 (zero)
Special: (none)
By: (leave blank)
Spacing Before: 6 pt
Spacing After: 6 pt
Line spacing: Match the selection for Normal
At: (leave blank)
Line and Page Breaks
Clear all boxes.
Click OK.

Next, click Format and from the dropdown menu select Font.

Font: Times New Roman (or) Courier/Courier New (or) Arial
Font Style: Regular
Size: 14pt
Click OK.
In the main task menu click OK.

For creative writing I recommend that you *do not* bold or italicize Headings. Definitely do not use a different font. It's unnecessary and can make extra work when it comes time to format an ebook or print-on-demand file. The same thing goes for automatic page and/or section breaks. They are unnecessary at this stage.

Heading 2, 3, etc.

Nonfiction might require additional Heading styles for subchapters and subheads. Word has built-in Heading styles up to level 9. Modify those styles the same way as for Heading 1, making certain the "Outline level" matches the Heading. Example: Heading 2 is Outline level 2. To make them easier to see while you write change the alignment, font size, and before and after spacing.

Now try it. In your sample doc insert a few chapter or section headers and apply Heading 1 to each of them by placing the cursor at the beginning of the text and clicking the style. That's how all your chapter and section starts will look from this point forward (until you modify the styles). No muss, no fuss, and no worrying about "formatting" when you should be thinking about what kind of torture to inflict on your hapless characters.

Applying Styles in an Existing Doc

Applying styles to a work in progress that hasn't been using styles at all, especially if the text was originally created in another program, can be a frustrating experience. If you've been using tabs or individually "formatting" paragraphs or have multiple fonts and have been using the space bar to align text, there will be conflicts in the underlying coding. Depending on the type of conflict, Word may or may not override the current formatting.

To find out if your work in progress will seamlessly accept new styling, do this:

1. Open a work in progress.
2. Save As to create a copy with a new file name.
3. Select all (Ctrl+a) the text.
4. Go to Home> Font and click the icon that looks like an A with an eraser: "Clear all formatting".
5. With the text still selected apply the Normal style by clicking on it.

If all your paragraphs are now styled in Normal, you're golden. Scroll through the doc and apply Heading 1 to chapter/section starts and your work in progress is ready for you to continue writing.

If, however, the doc is an uneven mess with styles applied haphazardly to some paragraphs, but not all, it means there is coding in the doc that Word is not recognizing or has a conflict with.

It means you have a bit of cleanup to do. Despite the number of steps, it won't take long.

STEP 1: Save As to make a copy and retain the original.

STEP 2: Get rid of tabs using Find and Replace:

Go to Home> Editing and click Replace to open the Find and Replace task menu.

> In the **Find** field: ^t
> In the **Replace** field: (leave it blank)
> **Replace All**

STEP 3: Turn soft returns into hard returns using Find and Replace:

> In the **Find** field: ^l (that's a lower case "L")
> In the **Replace** field: ^p
> **Replace All**

STEP 4: Tag italics using Find and Replace:

> In the **Find** field: Go to More> Format> Font and select Italic
> (leave the field blank)
> In the **Replace** field: -STARTI-^&-ENDI-
> **Replace All**

(Now all italics are wrapped in tags—absolutely necessary for the next few steps.)

STEP 5: Open a blank doc in a text editor such as Notepad. (Preloaded on the majority of Windows computers.)

STEP 6: Select all the text in the Word doc (Ctrl+a), copy it (Ctrl+c) and paste it (Ctrl+v) into the text editor.

STEP 7: Open a new blank doc in Word.

STEP 8: In the text editor, select all the text (Ctrl+a), copy it (Ctrl+c) and paste it (Ctrl+v) into the blank Word doc.

STEP 9: The entire doc should now be styled in Normal. Go through the doc and apply Heading 1 to chapter and section starts.

STEP 10: Restore italics using Find and Replace:
    Click "More" and click "Use wildcards"

> In the **Find** field: -STARTI-*-ENDI-
> In the **Replace** field: Go to More> Format> Font and select Italic (leave the field blank)
> **Replace All**

STEP 11: Delete the tags using Find and Replace:
    Clear "Use wildcards"

> In the **Find** field: -STARTI-
> In the **Replace** field: (leave blank, click No Formatting)
> **Replace All**

> In the **Find** field: -ENDI-
> In the **Replace** field: (leave blank)
> **Replace All**

If you have been using multiple hard returns (Enter) or holding down the space bar to align text, it's easy enough to get rid of all that unnecessary white space.

> Caution: If you have been using multiple hard returns to indicate scene breaks, now is the time to go through the doc and insert indicators so the scene breaks aren't lost. (## is my tag of choice for a scene break.)

STEP 1: In Home> Paragraph activate Show/Hide by clicking the ¶ icon.

STEP 2: Get rid of extra spaces using Find and Replace.
    (When I instruct you to use (space) it means hit the space bar once to create a blank space.)

In the **Find** field: (space)(space)
In the **Replace** field: (space)
Replace All and repeat until the results show zero matches.

STEP 3: Get rid of extra hard returns using Find and Replace.

In the **Find** field: ^p^p
In the **Replace** field: ^p
Replace All and repeat until the results show zero matches.

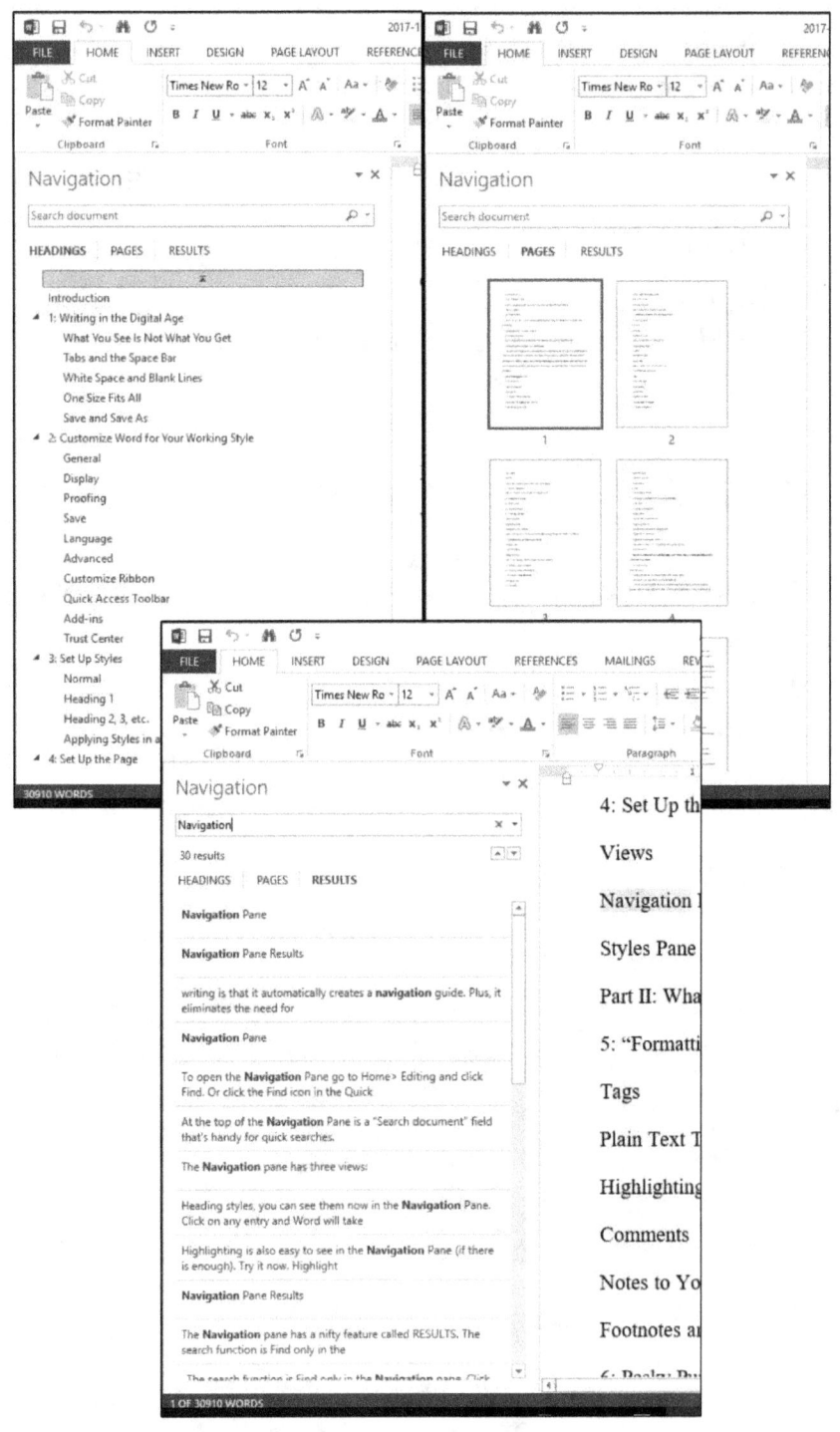

4: Set Up the Page

Views

Go to View> Views. Word offers multiple ways to view your doc.

The only time I use Print Layout view is when I'm formatting a doc for printing. For everything else I use Web Layout. Try it now. Switch the view from Print Layout to Web Layout and see the difference. Adjust the size of the window/screen and zoom in and out.

With Web Layout there are no margins to worry about. The screen size doesn't matter and there's rarely a worry about text being cut off and requiring the use of the horizontal scroll bar. Plus, it puts an end to obsessing about widows and orphans.

Navigation Pane

To open the Navigation Pane go to Home> Editing and click Find. Or click the Find icon in the Quick Access Toolbar—it looks like either binoculars or a magnifying glass.

At the top of the Navigation Pane is a "Search document" field that's handy for quick searches.

The Navigation pane has three views:

HEADINGS: Scrolling through a doc is so last century, not to mention an inefficient waste of time. If you have a doc open and have applied Heading styles, you can see them now in the Navigation Pane. Click on any entry and Word will take you to it. It doesn't matter if your novel has 12 chapters or 120, finding any of them is just a quick scroll and a click away. This also reduces the common error of misnumbering chapters.

PAGES: Displays thumbnails of the actual pages in a document. Handy for sneaking a peek at the page count if you're so inclined. Handier still while you're editing and you're looking for highlighted text.

RESULTS: Displays search results.

Styles Pane

To open the Styles Pane go to Home> Styles and click the arrow in the lower right corner.

The first time you open the Styles Pane it's going to display a long and probably confusing list; the length depends on whatever styles are in use or have been used or are in a particular Word template.

To change that, at the bottom of the pane is "Options…" Click it to open the task menu.

1. Select styles to show: "In use".
2. Select how the list is sorted: "As Recommended".
3. Check the boxes under "Select formatting to show as styles:" and clear the boxes under "Select how built-in style names are shown". Click on "New documents based on this template".
4. Click OK.

Now the Styles Pane shows only the styles you are using and it gives you a quick way to select a style rather than scrolling through the multiple options Word displays in the Home Ribbon.

To modify a style hover the cursor over the style name and right click to open the Modify Style task menu. To create a new style click on the Create a New Style icon located at the bottom left of the Styles Pane. In the chapters on formatting I'll show you how to easily create custom styles for specific projects.

PART II:

What To Do While You Write

=

Chapter One

"You poisoned my Nana."

Molly sank lower on the chair. She faced Blake Connor across a desk that looked as wide an ocean, but still wasn't big enough to hide her. She wanted to run from his office, shave her head, change her identity, and move to another country. She had known he was angry before she arrived at his office. It wasn't until she endured a solid five minutes of him glaring at her that she realized how angry he actually was.

Poisoned his Nana.[CHECK THIS]

Yes. Oh god. Yes, she had.

"I am so sorry, Mr. Connor. Truly truly sorry. I don't know what else to say. I refunded her money. I apologized to her and her friends. In person and in writing. It was an accident—"

"It was not an accident. It was negligence."

There was no room left to sink, other than to slide off the chair completely and curl up into a fetal ball on the floor.

She never should have taken the job in the first place. She wasn't a caterer. She didn't have a license. When Mrs. Connor, Blake Connor's grandmother, asked Molly's boss if Molly could provide desserts for her book club — "a dessert extravaganza" had been Mrs. Connor's exact words — Molly had been unable to resist.

Molly's boss had tried to resist. "We have not the catering license," he had told the elderly woman.

"Oh, I don't want catering, Mr. Knobb," Mrs. Connor had said. "I just want something elegant, unusual, exquisite, and guaranteed to put that silly Jennifer Arbogast in her place."

Herman Knobb had said, "We make you box lunches. Wonderful box lunches. We make them ready. You pick up. Tasty. Anything you want."

##

Mrs. Connor's face lit up with a mischievous sparkle. She was tall and thin and stiff-backed, but instead of looking severe the way so many tall, thin elderly women tended to look, Mrs. Connor always gave the impression of being on the verge of bursting into song. She said, "At the last meeting Jennifer Arbogast hired a sushi chef

13714 WORDS   140%

A novel in progress with the body styled in Normal;
the chapter heading styled in Heading 1.

The tag == indicates a page break.
The tag ## indicates a scene break.
Highlighted text in brackets is a note by the author to research a fact later.

5: "Formatting" on the Fly

Now you're writing a novel or short story or essay or article. The body of your work is set up in the Normal style and you're diligently applying the Heading styles to chapters and sections. You're working in Web Layout view so as not to be distracted by page breaks and margins and widows and orphans.

It's making you nervous.

How are you supposed to know where to insert page breaks?

How will anyone know there's a scene break?

What if you need special formatting because characters are sending text messages or emails? Reading newspaper headlines? Writing notes or letters?

What if you need bullet lists?

You might be tempted to create new styles while you're writing and apply them as you go. Or even use the Home> Paragraph quick formatting icons to center or offset text or create lists.

Don't do it.

Eventually you're going to have to clean the doc in order to prepare it for formatting and that will wipe out all that styling and you'll be back where you started, not knowing where the special formatting is supposed to go. In addition you don't want to inadvertently fill your doc with junk code that can create problems when it's shared with someone else.

Instead of "formatting" use Tags, Highlighting, Comments and Notes to Yourself.

And now you're really nervous. Don't be. You are working on a digital doc—fluid, flexible, easy to manipulate, easy to change. Until your words are fixed in a final form such as an ebook, print-on-demand book, or printed document, you can put in as many comments and tags as you need knowing you can easily delete them once they've fulfilled their purpose. Tags and comments are especially useful if you're hiring someone else to format your ebooks and print-on-demand editions. Let the formatter know you've left instructions for styling in the appropriate places and the pro will handle the rest.

Tags

Tags are search terms. I use them to quickly find page and section breaks, scene breaks and deliberate blank lines.

- For a page/section break: == (double equal sign)
- For a scene break: ## (double hashtag/pound sign)
- For a deliberate blank line: # (single hashtag/pound sign)

I've come up with these tags (and have used them for years) because:
a) equal signs and hashtags are not used widely in the types of docs I process;
b) they're easy to remember.
They aren't always appropriate—this book, for instance, uses the tags for examples and instructions and I don't want those mixed up with actual tags. If my tags don't work for you, come up with your own.

- Make tags unique so they are easy to search for without having to sort hundreds of results throughout the body of text. Example: "ppp" for page breaks; "***" for scene break; "dbl" for a deliberate blank line.
- Make them easy to remember so it's easy to get into the habit of using them.
- Always place tags on their own line. That gives you an additional means of searching for them using Find and for replacing or deleting them using Find and Replace when it comes time to format.

Plain Text Tags

For blocks of text that will eventually require special formatting—correspondence, newspaper headlines, poetry, text messages, emails, lists, etc.—use plain text tags.
Some examples:
[NOTE] [END NOTE]

[TEXT MSG] [END TEXT MSG]
[POEM] [END POEM]
[BULLET LIST] [END LIST]

How it looks in a doc:
>[NOTE]
>Jenny,
>I love you and please don't ever fix meatloaf for supper again.
>Love,
>Michael
>[END NOTE]

It doesn't matter what the tag says as long as you know what it means.

Notice my tags are in all caps. It makes them easy to see—they really do seem to jump off the screen. It also makes them easier to search for. In Find> More check the "Match case" option and that way you can search for only all caps tags.

Notice, too, the square brackets. Square brackets [ ] are rare in fiction and rarely overused in nonfiction. They make an excellent search term. When I'm ready to format, I search for [and it will find all the plain text tags.

★

A word about lists, either bulleted or numbered. Word creates lists very well. Ebooks render simple (single level) lists very well. In a print edition, the sky is the limit with lists. Despite how easy it is to click on the icon for a list, *don't do it* while you're writing. The reason why is because when the doc is cleaned, the process will remove the list styling, but the bullets or numbers or letters will remain, along with the tabs Word uses. So you'll have to remove them in order to properly format the lists. It's easier to tag them while writing.

Highlighting

To highlight text, go to Home> Font. Select the text you want highlighted and click the icon that looks like ab with a highlighter pen. The default color is neon yellow.

Let's say a bit of dialogue is giving you fits or you realize some research is required. Rather than stop writing, highlight the troublesome passage and keep on writing.

Let's say you're inserting editorial changes into a doc, but you're undecided and want some time to think about it. Highlight the text to deal with later.

Highlights can be searched for. In Find and Replace go to More> Format> Highlight. Word will find every instance no matter what color highlighting is used.

Highlighting is also easy to see in the Navigation Pane (if there is enough). Try it now. Highlight a paragraph then switch the view to PAGES. The highlighting jumps right out at you.

The downside is that unlike tags highlighting does not survive a doc cleaning. Anything you highlight needs to be addressed and dealt with before the doc is cleaned.

Comments

Go to Insert> Comments *or* Review> Comments> New Comments to create a new comment. Try it now. A box will open on the right side of the screen and you can type in a reminder for yourself or another reader.

There are downsides to using the comment feature:

- The markup area uses up screen space.
- Depending on what type of computer and/or program a recipient is using, not everyone you share the doc with will be able to read the comments.
- Comments will not survive the doc cleaning process.

To get rid of comments go to Review> Comments. Click the Next icon to go from comment to comment. Delete once they've been addressed. To delete them all at once, click the arrow under the Delete icon and click "Delete all comments in Document".

Notes to Yourself

If you wish to retain comments after the doc is cleaned in preparation for formatting, write notes to yourself.

Examples:

[INSERT IMAGE toodles.jpeg CAPTION "Baby waves bye-bye to Daddy"]

[INSERT HORIZONTAL RULE]

[OFFSET PARAGRAPH]

If you'll be sending the doc to a professional formatter, use notes like these to let the formatter know your preferences. And make sure to tell the formatter what to look for.

Notice the square brackets, again. They are a handy dandy, multi-purpose search term.

Footnotes and Endnotes

Word makes it easy as sneezing to insert footnotes and endnotes.

Set the cursor in the referenced text. Go to References> Footnotes. Click the icon for footnotes or endnotes and insert the note.

If you are creating a doc to print immediately—a term paper, for instance—foot- and endnote away. If your intent, however, is to share the file or publish it, footnotes and endnotes require special handling.

Footnotes and endnotes will not survive the cleaning process intact. If sent to a professional formatter, the formatter will have to recover the text for special treatment, increasing the chance of errors, and if the formatter charges hourly rates, that's additional cost.

The best way to handle them is to:

1. Make a note in the doc for the reference points: [FOOTNOTE 1] or [ENDNOTE 1]
2. Write the reference material in a separate doc with notes about placement: [CHAPTER 4, FOOTNOTE 1]
3. When it is time to format for a specific purpose, copy/paste the foot- and endnote material from the separate doc into the formatted doc.

6: Pesky Punctuation

Em Dashes

This punctuation mark trips up writers all the time. In docs I receive from clients—and in ebooks and even in print—I see en dashes instead of em dashes, single, double or triple dashes instead of em dashes, and quite often a confusing mixture throughout.

The easiest way of all to create em dashes is to activate AutoCorrect.

1. Go to Insert> Symbols> More Symbols> AutoCorrect...
2. In the task menu click on "Replace text as you type".
3. Click the "Formatted text" box.
4. From the list select the suggestion to turn a double dash -- into an em dash.
5. Click OK.

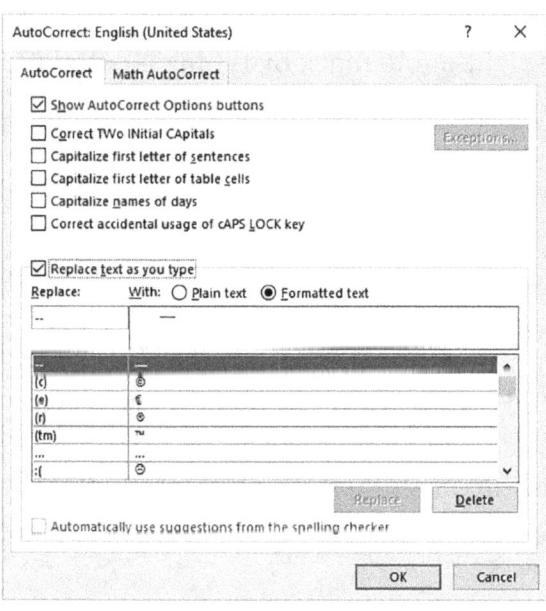

Caution: Be judicious in your use of AutoCorrect and AutoFormat. There's nothing more annoying than to be blazing away at the speed of sound and having Word coming along behind you fixing things you might not want it to fix.

There are hotkeys in Word to allow the quick insertion of either an em or en dash. Ctrl+alt+- (minus on the number keypad) inserts an em dash. Ctrl+- (minus on the number keypad) inserts an en dash.

You can also manually insert em and en dashes via the Insert> Symbol> Special Characters menu.

If you're in the middle of a project and need to change the double dashes into em dashes, use Find and Replace.

In the **Find** field: --
In the **Replace** field: ^+
Replace All

One thing Word does that drives me crazy (along with most fiction writers, I'm sure) is this:

—"

or this

--"

It places a left double or single quote mark after a dash (em, en or single). I have yet to figure out a way to convince the program that it is perfectly acceptable to end dialogue with an em dash and thus it requires a right double or single quote mark.

One way to fix them is to do a search for dashes paired with quote marks to make sure they are turned the right way.

While writing, force Word to use the right quote mark by typing a letter after the dash like this:

—a"

then delete the letter so you end up with this

—"

Ellipsis

An ellipsis looks like three periods, but is actually a character. It can be used in conjunction with a period, comma, or question mark.

The easiest way to turn three periods into an ellipsis is to activate the option in AutoCorrect to automatically replace three periods with an ellipsis while you write.

1. Go to Insert> Symbols> More Symbols> AutoCorrect...
2. In the task menu click on "Replace text as you type".
3. Click the "Formatted text" box.
4. From the list select the suggestion to turn three periods into an ellipsis.
5. Click OK.

You can also use a hot key: Alt+Ctrl+. (that's a period)

To use Find and Replace, first activate AutoCorrect to replace three periods with an ellipsis. Then:

> In the **Find** field: ... (three periods)
> In the **Replace** field: ... (three periods)
> **Replace All**

Single and Double Quote Marks, and Apostrophes

I usually disable AutoCorrect and AutoFormat, with one exception: Smart quotes (curly quotes). I do this for two reasons:

1. In HTML and CSS straight quotes are restricted characters that can adversely affect ebooks;
2. Straight quotes look unprofessional in a commercial product.

To convert straight quotes to curly/smart quotes in an existing document, go to File> Options> Proofing> AutoCorrect options...> AutoFormat. Click on smart quotes.

Next, use Find and Replace for double quotes.

> In the **Find** field: "
> In the **Replace** field: "
> **Replace All**

Word will automatically replace all the straight double quotes with curly double quotes. After this is done, check for any instances of a dash closed by a quote mark and fix as necessary.

Use Find and Replace for single quotes.

> In the **Find** field: '
> In the **Replace** field: '
> **Replace All**

Be aware that Word doesn't distinguish between an apostrophe and a single quote mark. This is a problem in the case of open contractions, which Word doesn't understand at all. "Get 'em!" "Rock 'n' roll." "How 'bout them Yankees?" "He looked great back in the '60s." Open contractions require an apostrophe *not* a left single quote.

While writing type

a'em

to force Word to use an apostrophe, then delete the a to end up with

'em.

7: Special Characters

What about characters with diacritical marks: acute accent; grave accent; tilde; macron; breve; etc.? What about symbols for copyright and trademark?

Go to Insert> Symbols> More Symbols and select the desired character from the character menu. A double-click inserts it in the doc.

This presents a special problem. The Symbols menu contains special characters and supplemental tables for *every font installed on your computer*—including characters you weren't even aware were on your computer such as Greek or Cyrillic or Arabic. That isn't a big problem if you intend to print the doc yourself on your home computer. It can be a *huge* problem when it's time to share the doc or format an ebook.

The safest of the safe characters are limited to ASCII (hex). That's the basic language of email programs and ebook reading devices. Most email programs and e-ink reading devices, tablets and smartphones are capable of rendering a wide range of Unicode symbols, but some older devices cannot. In the lower right of the Symbols menu is a field for "from:" In the dropdown menu select ASCII (hex). The subset option for supplemental tables disappears.

That said, programs and ebook reading devices are constantly being updated and refined. A Unicode character that failed to render yesterday might very well be useful today. Call the ASCII (hex) selection the "Safe" selection with never a problem, and call Unicode "Try it and See."

I'll cover special characters in the chapters on formatting with tips for figuring out if a character is suitable for use.

⁒ ★ ⁓

Word has a handy feature: a quick access menu containing recently used special characters. Let's say you've written the word "naïve". You inserted the small letter i with a diaeresis from the Symbols menu. The next time you need that character, click the arrow next to Symbol and the character will be in the dropdown menu. One click will insert it. The quick access menu displays up to twenty characters, more than enough for most writing projects.

Another way to insert special characters is to use shortcut keys. In the Symbols menu click on a character to highlight it. At the bottom of the menu is the shortcut key: Alt+(a code).

Example: The shortcut key for a small letter i with a diaeresis is Alt+0239. Hold down the Alt key and type in the numbers. Try it now.

One way to use those efficiently would be to create a list of shortcut keys for the characters you know you'll be using often and post the list for quick reference while you write.

Another method is to create your own shortcut keys. For instance, I just created one for the ï character: Ctrl+i

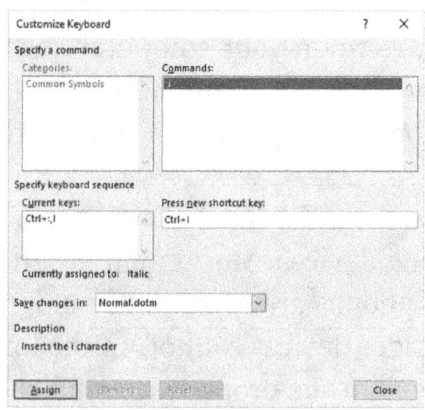

To do this go to Insert> Symbols> Symbol> More Symbols to open the menu. Click on a character to highlight it. Click "Shortcut Key..." This opens a new task menu: Customize Keyboard. The symbol you want to shortcut will appear in the gray area under "Press new shortcut key:" If there is a current key, it will appear in the "Current keys:" field. Enter a new command in the "Press new shortcut key:" field. Make your command Ctrl plus something. (Word disallows some commands and will not allow you to override other shortcuts already in use.) Save changes either in Word or in your current doc. Click "Assign" and the shortcut key is live. Create a cheat sheet to make it easy to remember what you've created.

Word offers hotkeys and shortcuts for commonly used special characters such as the copyright mark ©. Go to Insert> Symbol> Special Characters. There is a list of special characters to choose from.

Or click the AutoCorrect button to open a customization menu. Check the box for "Replace text as you type". As an example, from the list select the copyright symbol and double-click to place it in the "Replace" and "With" fields. Click OK. Now when you type (c) Word will autocorrect it to ©.

Caution: AutoCorrect and AutoFormat in Word can be as annoying and goof-producing as autocorrect on a phone. Unless you have a razor-sharp memory and are a very careful typist, use these features judiciously.

My preferred method is to use Find and Replace. While I'm writing I type, for example, "naive" and make a note of it in my style sheet.* When I'm finished with the project and ready for editorial work, I'll have a list of words requiring special characters. I'll use Find to search for the first instance of "naive" and correct it. Copy/paste "naïve" into the Replace field. Then use Find Next to go through the doc, making corrections where necessary.

* *Style sheets* are different from Styles. I'll explain them in Chapter 8: Create a Style Sheet.

PART III:

What To Do After the Writing is Done

8: Create a Style Sheet

You've typed "The End" and your novel or short story or essay is ready for editing.

Whether you're experienced enough to self-edit, or the intent is to send it off to an editor, or even submit it to a publishing house, an essential tool is a style sheet.

If your intent is to self-publish, that makes *you* the publisher and every publisher needs a house style in order to maintain consistency in a catalog of works.

Style sheets aren't a Word feature, but rather a tool to help you create a written work that is consistent and professional. It's immensely helpful during the editing process, not only for you but for hired editors and/or proofreaders.

> Note: A style sheet is different from a **style manual**. A style manual covers rules of grammar, punctuation and capitalization, when and where to use italics or quotes, and rules for structuring quoted material and bibliographies. Manuals are available as dense tomes such as *The Chicago Manual of Style* or as light guides such as Strunk & White's *Elements of Style*. There are many, many online resources, some paid and some free. Pick one that suits your writing and consider it your "authority". Make it your go-to assistant in all matters grammatical.

A style sheet can be created in Word, or in a text editor, or in a spreadsheet. There are programs such as OneNote. Style sheets can carry over from one writing project to another and are essential for anyone writing a series.

Typical entries in a style sheet:

- Character names (Is she Christy or Kristy or Christie?)*
- Place names

- Product names
- Spelling preferences (judgement or judgment?)
- Capitalization rules
- Foreign words with special characters
- Made up words

> * This comes in handy if you're making up character names on the fly. A glance at the style sheet reveals you've inadvertently given all your secondary characters names that begin with "R" or somehow you've included a John, Jack, Jonny, Jay and Joanne; or a William, Will, Willie, Bill, and Billie. Might want to fix that.

A style sheet will save you much time and energy during editing and proofreading. Hired editors and proofreaders will have a handy reference and that cuts down on phone calls and emails. If you're writing a series, questions might arise such as "What was that little town in Book 2—Johnstown? Jonestown?" A glance at the style sheet gives you the answer.

A useful habit: While writing, highlight any item that belongs in the style sheet. At the end of the day's writing session, copy/paste the highlighted material into the style sheet. It's like keeping a running tab.

9: Spell Check

Find spell check in Review> Proofing> Spelling & Grammar.

The best tip for its use is to always remember this: Spell check is a tool, not an authority.

It has its limits.

For instance:

Compound words using hyphens, or words that are sometimes one word and sometimes two. Spell check is an unreliable source when it comes to whether or not any particular word should be hyphenated, or hyphenated in some instances and not in others; ditto for words that are sometimes split. Language evolves and many words that used to be hyphenated no longer are. Use an up-to-date dictionary or a reliable online source.

Homonyms. Spell check isn't going to say you've used "hanger" incorrectly when you actually meant "hangar"; it'll only tell you whether you've spelled it correctly or not. The same goes for not quite right words. You mean to write "collegiate" but actually wrote "collegial" and spell check will report that everything is okay.

Product names. Many brand names are trademarked. Some companies are very aggressive about protecting their trademarks and it's not unheard of for an author to receive a cease & desist letter or take-down notice because of trademark misuse, including misspelling. (Trademark protection is 100% the responsibility of the trademark owner and failure to protect can mean a brand name can fall into common usage, no longer trademarked.) Writers have a responsibility to research product names to find out: a) proper spelling and capitalization; b) if a trademark symbol is required; c) if the use of the name requires special wording, i.e. "Coca-Cola brand soft drink". As the publisher, you have the responsibility of checking all product names and ensuring they are either used correctly or not used at all.

⟋ ★ ⟍

One feature that is especially helpful for fiction writers is the "Add" a word to the dictionary feature. If, as suggested above, you've created a style sheet, you'll have a list of names, places and unusual words and, in the case of fantasy/science fiction, invented words. When it comes time to run a spell check, copy/paste the list from the style sheet into the top of your doc. When spell check flags a word in that list, add it to the dictionary. That way, spell check will recognize that Gandalf (for example) is the correct spelling of a character's name, but will flag typos such as Gandolf.

Go to File> Options> Proofing to customize spell check and add dictionaries.

10: Track Changes

Track Changes is one of Word's more useful features. It allows you and/or your editor to mark up a document with editorial comments and make changes in the doc while retaining the original text.

When using Track Changes, it is easier to work in Print Layout view. Go to View> Views to select it.

Track Changes is found in Review> Tracking.

Before using Track Changes do a Save As and create a new doc so that your original remains untouched—just in case.

Activate Track Changes by clicking on the icon. To open the options menu click on the arrow in the lower right hand corner of the Review> Tracking box. Set your preferences.

When choosing options, remember, Track Changes was designed with an office environment in mind. Drone 1 types up a report and sends it to Drones 2, 3, and 4 for input, and then it's sent to Boss 1, who then sends it to Boss 2, and so on. A self-publisher might have one or two editors, or no editor at all. Choose only those options that make editing easier for you.

Choose *how much* markup is displayed on the screen: All Markup; Simple Markup; No Markup; and Original. Some writers want to see everything they do, some want to see very little.

Choose *what* to display in the dropdown menu under Show Markup. One of the options is Balloons. Activating Balloons will create boxes to appear on the right hand side of the screen. Balloons has a submenu to choose which changes are displayed.

The Reviewing Pane has two options: Vertical, which opens a viewing pane on the left hand side of the screen that shows all changes made; Horizontal, which opens a pane at the bottom of the screen to show the changes.

What's the best display? Depends on the writer. Try this now: Open a new blank document and either type in a few dummy paragraphs or copy/paste some text from a work in progress into the doc. Activate Track Changes and try out the different viewing options. Figure out what meets your needs. The point is to not be so frustrated, flustered, or distracted by what is happening on the screen that you give up on Track Changes altogether.

After the editing process, use Accept or Reject to either insert or delete a change. If you trust all the changes and don't have a need to go through the changes one by one, you can select "Accept all changes and Stop tracking". Or, if you don't want any changes, select "Reject all changes and Stop tracking".

Caution: It is vitally important that you make sure all changes are either accepted or rejected and that Track Changes is OFF before formatting a commercial product such as an ebook or print-on-demand edition. Otherwise, extraneous text and other weirdness can end up peppered throughout the book.

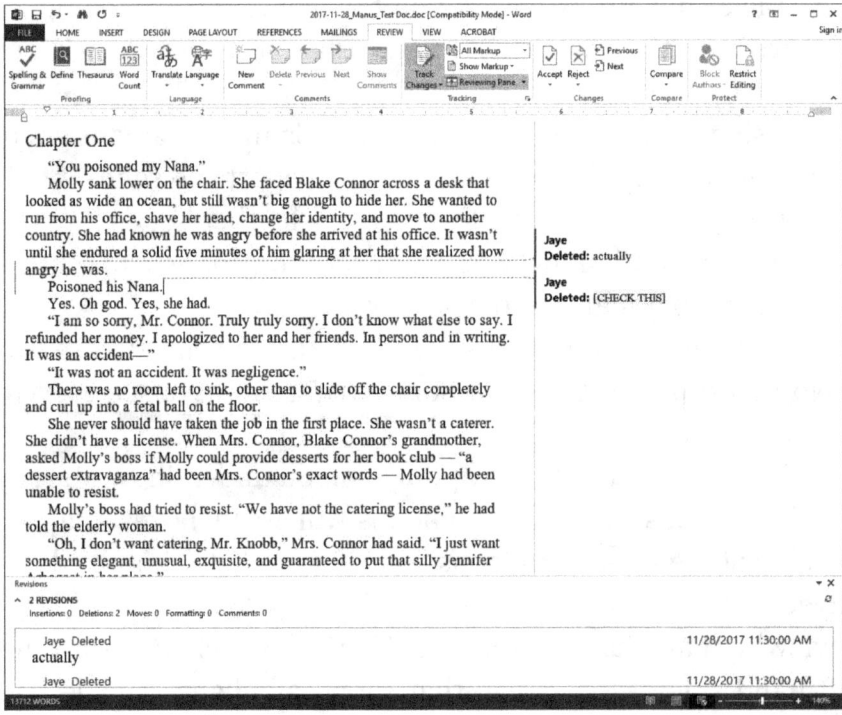

Track Changes with revisions shown in balloons
and in the horizontal viewing pane.

11: Find and Replace

Word's search function is excellent and powerful, turning many otherwise tedious tasks into one- or two-step operations. Once you understand how it works, it'll become your favorite tool.

How it works: It finds *exactly* what you tell it to find and will replace it with *exactly* what you tell it to replace.

Most writers I know underuse Find and Replace without ever realizing what a terrific tool it is during editorial processes. It can find special characters, special formatting, fonts, styles, and highlighted text. It can find hard and soft paragraph returns, page breaks and section breaks. It can find formatting tags and notes to yourself.

Search Options

Go to Home> Editing and click Replace to open the Find and Replace menu. Click More to reveal Search Options. Each one of those options refines a find and a replace operation.

For instance, to find Apple the company but not apple the fruit, check "MATCH CASE", type "Apple" into the Find field and results will show Apple only when it is capitalized.

Check "FIND WHOLE WORDS ONLY" if searching for a word such as "able" but don't want results for constable, disable, or usable.

"FIND ALL WORD FORMS" can be useful—especially if you're prone to what I call "stupidities of choice." That's where, in the heat of creation, you blast through a draft, writing as fast as you can, but afterward, with a cooler eye, you discover all your characters are blinking as if having an allergy attack, or crossing their arms, or otherwise repeating an action. Search for "blink" (for example) and the matches will include blink, blinked, and blinking. Search for "judge" and results will show judged, judgment, and judging.

"SOUNDS LIKE (ENGLISH)" is a feature more writers should use because it can track down homonyms. When I edit or proofread, if I run across a homonym mix-up such as "mantle" (a cloak) when the writer meant "mantel" (a shelf for a fireplace), I'll do a search with "Sounds like" activated and the results will give me every instance of both mantle and mantel, and I can check each usage for accuracy.

"USE WILDCARDS" gets into regex territory, which, in general is far more sophisticated than any writer needs. To access the wildcard commands, in Find and Replace> More check the "Use wildcards" box. Click Special and that brings up a list of wildcard commands. The command I use the most is the asterisk "*", which tells Word to find any string of characters within certain parameters. Try it yourself to see what I mean. Check the "Use wildcards" box and in the Find field type a*e and click Find. The matches will include every string of characters that begins with "a" and ends with "e".

The most common typo I see (and make myself) is mixing up "it's" and "its", which also happens to be easy to miss during a proofread. To run a quick check, check the boxes "Find whole words only" *and* "Ignore punctuation characters".

In the **Find** field: it's

Word will find every instance of it's (contraction), its (possessive), and its' (mistake). These Find options are also good ways to check for apostrophe placement in possessives. Do you mean "Smith's house" or "the Smiths' house"? Run a search to check that apostrophes are where they belong.

"MATCH PREFIX" and "MATCH SUFFIX" options instruct Word to find only those strings of characters that come at the beginnings or the ends of words. Suppose you have trouble remembering which "pro" prefix requires a hyphen and which does not. Rather than stop writing to look it up, wait until you are in edit mode and search for every instance of "pro" as a prefix and check. Perhaps it's been pointed out that you're a little too fond of adverbs, especially modifiers that end in "ly"—merrily, happily, grouchily, etc.-ly. Do a suffix search for "ly".

Replace Options

At the bottom left of the Find and Replace menu are three boxes: Format, Special, and No Formatting.

Even though they are shown under "Replace", you can use many of these options for *either* searching or replacing.

FORMAT: In the dropdown menu are options for searching and replacing fonts, paragraphs, styles and highlights.

FORMAT> FONT opens a menu box where you can refine a search to a specific font family, font size, and font style (regular, italic, bold). You can also search for underlining, and special effects such as color.

FORMAT> PARAGRAPH finds specific paragraph formatting, such as line indents and line spacing.

FORMAT> STYLES allows you to quickly find and replace styles. When this menu is opened it will list every single style available in your version of Word, including Word's templates and your custom styles. Each style has a code:
¶ = paragraph style
a = character style
¶a = paragraph and character style
▪- = list style

FORMAT> HIGHLIGHT allows you to find or replace highlighted text.

FORMAT> TABS. As noted in Chapter 1, tabs are troublemakers. If your work contains tabs it's easy to get rid of them.

> In the **Find** field: ^t
> In the **Replace** field: (leave it blank)
> **Replace All**

REPLACE> SPECIAL. Invaluable for finding special characters and codes both seen and unseen. Here you can find and replace em and en dashes, hard and soft line returns, page and section breaks, and discretionary hyphens.

Copy/Paste in Find and Replace. Unfortunately, Word disallows inserting characters directly from the Symbols menu into the Find and Replace fields. It will allow some shortcut keys, but not all of them. (And I've yet to break the code on how it determines which characters to allow.) It's easier to copy/paste text directly from the doc into the Find and Replace fields. For example, you've been typing "cafe" while you compose, but now you want to use "café". Find the first instance of "cafe" in your doc, manually change it to "café" then copy/paste "café" into the Replace field and use Find Next to go through the doc until you've fixed all instances.

Another time to use copy/paste is when you need to find a smart quote (double or single quote). Merely typing " or ' into the Find field will result in every double or single quote in the doc. By copy/pasting a left or right double or single quote into the Find field along with spaces according to grammatical rules, the search is narrowed considerably.

White Space. Find and Replace treats white space as a search or replace string. A common error is to inadvertently insert a space or inadvertently omit a space in the Find or Replace fields. If you're searching for something you know is in the doc but results keep coming up zero, check the white space.

REPLACE ALL: Replace All can make some tasks as easy and quick as a few mouse clicks. It can also create major headaches. Unless your search terms are unique, be cautious about using Replace All.

If you inadvertently click Replace All when all you wanted to do was Replace one item, use Undo (the icon at the top of the toolbar looks like a turning arrow) or Ctrl+z.

Navigation Pane Results

The Navigation pane has a nifty feature called RESULTS. The search function is Find only in the Navigation pane. Click on Results, type a search term into the Find field, and Results will display every instance of the search term, the number of times it is used, and offer a snippet of text in which the term appears.

(Unless there are too many results for the program to display. In that case Results will display "That shows up a lot!")

Results can determine if you've overused an action or a descriptor. For an example, you suspect a character is saying "Good Gawd Almighty" too often. Or maybe there is a lot of scratching of noses or nodding of heads going on. Search for whatever is bugging you and look at the results. It's easy to scroll through Results in order to pick and choose which instances you want to change and which to leave alone.

PART IV

What to do When the Writing and Editing are Done but Before Formatting

12: Scrub the Doc of Extraneous Coding

The doc is edited, revised and polished. It's ready for formatting for a specific purpose: submission, ebook, Advance Reading Copy, print-on-demand edition, or even a hard copy manuscript. Before you proceed the doc *must be* scrubbed clean to remove extraneous and/or destructive coding. Even if you've followed all my recommendations and used Normal and Heading styles for a work in progress, it's easy to inadvertently insert destructive coding.

In the case of digital formatting, much of the coding that Word produces isn't recognized by ebook conversion programs and will be ignored. In some cases it causes conflicts that cannot be overridden or ignored and that can damage the ebook or cause it to fail to convert.

You will need a text editor for this process—any program capable of generating a bare-bones, no formatting .txt file. If using a Windows PC, the computer most likely came pre-installed with NotePad. NotePad is sufficient for what you need to do. On a Mac, TextEdit will work.

> Note: Word can generate a .txt (Plain text) file, but it's not useful for this purpose. Word inserts a lot of extraneous code into its .txt files that would have to be cleaned out and so it defeats the purpose of what needs doing.

★

Many writers balk at doc cleaning. They get flustered by the many steps and by having to use another program in conjunction with Word. Even so, it's even more frustrating when an ebook fails conversion; or to be laying out a doc for a print-on-demand book and having to do battle with locked coding; or to have someone with whom you've shared a file through email tell you they can't read your doc; or to receive a complaint from a reader (or many readers) about formatting flaws in your ebook.

If you've been using styles and tags, and have refrained from junking up your doc with "formatting" as you write, this cleaning process will take maybe fifteen or twenty minutes. Once you've done it a few times, it'll be second nature.

Start in Word

STEP 1: Save As to make a copy to retain the original doc.

STEP 2: Deactivate Track Changes. If Track Changes was used, accept or reject *all* changes and turn off Track Changes. Do this in one step by clicking the dropdown menu under either the Accept or Reject icon and choosing "Accept all changes and Stop Tracking" or "Reject all changes and Stop Tracking".

STEP 3: Comments and Highlighted Text. Comments created using the comment feature in Word will *not* survive the cleaning process. If you need to retain comments, go to Review> Comments> Next to find each comment. Copy/paste the comment text directly into the document and tag it with square brackets.
Example: [this is the text from the comment]
Search for highlights either by scrolling through PAGES in the Navigation Pane, or use Find and Replace:

> In the **Find** field: More> Format Highlight (leave the field blank)
> Use **Find Next** to find each instance.

Deal with whatever is highlighted or turn it into a note to yourself.

STEP 4: Activate Show. The Show/Hide feature is found in Home> Paragraph. The icon is a pilcrow: ¶. Click the icon and you'll be able to see paragraph returns, soft returns, tabs, spaces and other formatting.

STEP 5: Remove Tabs and Soft Returns.
Tabs are troublemakers in any type of digital format. Soft returns, for the most part, are troublemakers, too. Use Find and Replace to remove tabs and soft returns.

> ¶
> → ·"I·won't.·I·want·revenge,·Ms.·Larsen.·I·want·my·pound·of·flesh."¶
> → → Molly·mentally·tallied·all·she·owned.·She·owed·the·bank·for·her·car.· She'd·inherited·her·house,·but·Blake·Connor's·suits·were·probably·worth·more·than· her·entire·property,·including·her·second-hand·furnishings.·What·little·she·had·in·the· bank·was·squirreled·away·in·a·fund·to·pay·for·culinary·school.·Her·wages·from·the· restaurant·were·enough·to·live·on,·barely.¶
> ¶
> He·leaned·forward·and·gave·her·an·up·and·down·look·that·felt·like·a·hot·iron· grazing·her·skin.↵
> ···························"You·look·like·you·could·spare·a·pound.·Or·two."↵
> ¶
> "Hey!"¶
> A·faint·smile,·but·not·a·pleasant·one.·Molly·sensed·she·wasn't·going·to·like· whatever·was·coming·next.¶
> "Look,·Mr.·Connor,·I'm·sorry.·I·am·so·so·deeply·and·truly·sorry.·It·was· negligence.·I·had·no·business·catering.·I'll·never·do·it·again.·You·have·my·promise·on· that.·But·what·do·you·want·from·me?·How·can·I·make·this·up·to·you?·I·don't·have· much·money.·I—"¶
> "Are·you·married,·Ms.·Larsen?"————————Section Break (Next Page)————————
> ¶

Show Activated to display page and section breaks, tabs, spaces, paragraph returns and soft returns.

To delete tabs:

 In the **Find** field: ^t
 In the **Replace** field: (leave blank)
 Replace All and repeat until the results show no matches

To change soft returns into hard returns:

 In the **Find** field: ^l (that is a lower case "L")
 In the **Replace** field: ^p
 Replace All

STEP 6: Tag Page Breaks and Section Breaks.

If page or section breaks were used they will vanish during cleaning, but depending on the text editing program it could create artefact characters you may or may not see when the text is returned to Word. Whether you see them or not, they can cause problems. Use Find and Replace to tag breaks.

To tag page breaks:

> In the **Find** field: ^m
> In the **Replace** field: ^p==^p
> **Replace All**

If the project requires section breaks along with page breaks, tag them with plain text so they don't get mixed up with page breaks.

> In the **Find** field: ^b
> In the **Replace** field: ^p[SECTION]^p
> **Replace All**

STEP 7: Blank Lines. Ensure all deliberate blank lines are tagged as recommended in Chapter 5. *This step is vitally important.* In the next step you'll be getting rid of all extraneous blank lines. If you skip *this* step you'll lose stanza spacing in poetry, or the blank lines before and after a special paragraph such as for correspondence. It's also important to know where your scene breaks should be.

Use Find and Replace to find extra hard returns.

> In the **Find** field: ^p^p
> Use **Find Next** to find each instance

As you find each result, tag it or insert a comment so you know what the blank line is for. If the blank line is unnecessary, skip it. It'll be deleted in the next step.

STEP 8: Extraneous White Space.

Line spacing in digital *and* print is enough of a headache in book production without creating extra hassles with unnecessary spaces between words and sentences, and at the beginnings and ends of paragraphs. Delete them with Find and Replace.

Note: (space) means hitting the space bar to create a blank space in the Find or Replace field.

Remove extra spaces within paragraphs:

> In the **Find** field: (space)(space)
> In the **Replace** field: (space)
> **Replace All** and repeat until the results show no matches

Remove extra spaces at the beginnings of paragraphs:

> In the **Find** field: ^p(space)
> In the **Replace** field: ^p
> **Replace All** and repeat until the results show no matches

Remove extra spaces at the ends of paragraphs:

> In the **Find** field: (space)^p
> In the Replace field ^p
> **Replace All** and repeat until the results show no matches

Remove unnecessary blank lines:

> In the **Find** field: ^p^p
> In the **Replace** field: ^p
> **Replace All** and repeat until the results show no matches

STEP 9: Tag the Headings.

If your novel or narrative nonfiction has the usual chapter or section designations, Chapter 1, Chapter 2, etc., this step is optional. (You already have a built-in search term and dealing with ten or twenty headings manually doesn't take long. It's also easy to search for page break or section break tags.)

If, however, you have 50 or 70 or 150 chapters or your copy contains multiple heading styles, tagging them at this stage will make restoring them easy.

There is one downside to using Find and Replace for Heading styles: Word will sometimes drop the end/close tag to the next line, like this:

-H1-Chapter One
-ENDH1-It was a dark and stormy night . . .

The upside is that you will be able to *see* it and fix it.

Use Find and Replace to tag Heading 1*:

> In the **Find** field: Format> Styles> Heading 1 (leave the field blank)
> In the **Replace** field: -H1-^&-ENDH1-
> **Replace All**

> * When the list of Styles is opened, Word will include every style in its library. There may be multiple Heading styles listed. Click on a style and Word will display its styling so that before you click OK you can ensure the style is the one you want.

To tag other Heading styles, use these terms to wrap the Headings:
Heading 2: -H2- -ENDH2-
Heading 3: -H3- -ENDH3-
And so on.
If the end/close tags have been dropped to the next line as in the above example, fix that now.

> In the **Find** field: ^p-ENDH1- (or -ENDH2-, -ENDH3-, etc.)
> In the **Replace** field: -ENDH1-^p (or -ENDH2-, -ENDH3-, etc.)
> **Replace All**

STEP 10: Tag Special Formatting.
Italics, bolding and underlining will disappear when the text is copy/pasted into the text editor. They must be wrapped in tags in order to retain them. Use Find and Replace.

To tag italics:

> In the **Find** field: More> Format> Font Italic (leave the field blank)
> In the **Replace** field: -STARTI-^&-ENDI-
> **Replace All**

To tag bolded text:

> In the **Find** field: More> Format> Font Bold (leave the field blank)
> In the **Replace** field: -STARTB-^&-ENDB-
> **Replace All**

To tag underlining:

> In the **Find** field: More> Format> Font Underline (leave the field blank)
> In the **Replace** field: -STARTU-^&-ENDU-
> **Replace All**

> Note: You might be wondering about the tags. I use many different programs in my daily work and so I had to devise tags that are program neutral and will be retained no matter what program I'm using and will not cause problems in Find and Replace operations. In order to use Replace All safely, it's vital the tags not be mistaken for regular text. Hence, the use of all caps and dashes.

STEP 11: Punctuation Check.

If you're confident of your punctuation, skip this step. Otherwise, refer back to Chapter 6: Pesky Punctuation and make sure dashes, ellipses and quote marks are all up to standard.

STEP 12: Tag Extra Special Character Formatting.

If your project requires footnotes, endnotes, superscript or subscript characters, colored text, small caps, larger or smaller characters, or other special effects, make sure the instances are noted with plain text tags so you can easily find them again.

STEP 13: Hyphenation.

Not the single dash for hyphenating compound words, but optional hyphens for aligning text on a line. If for some reason you've been hyphenating while you write, select all the text (Ctrl+a), go to Page Layout > Page Layout> Hyphenation and click on the down arrow. Click None to turn off the hyphenation. If you're still seeing hyphens (and it might be my version of Word or that Word in general is loathe to get rid of hyphens, but sometimes they won't go away!) use Find and Replace to get rid of them:

> In the **Find** field: ^-
> In the **Replace** field: (leave it blank)
> **Replace All**

If any part of your text has been restored via OCR (Optical Character Recognition) or imported from a publishing program, hyphens might be present but invisible. A search for Optional Hyphens will not produce results because Word will have inserted an invisible "Not Sign" character.

The *visible* "Not Sign" looks like this: ¬ That is also the Optional Hyphen character, but the two act differently.

Sometimes, you can make them appear in the doc. Go to File> Options> Display and check the box for Optional Hyphen.

If turning on the Show Optional Hyphen feature lets you see ¬ in the text, copy/paste the character into the Find field and use Replace All to delete all instances.

Otherwise, wait until the text is copy/pasted into a text editor (where they *will* show up). There you can do a Find and Replace All to delete the "Not Sign" characters.

The Text Editor

STEP 1: Open a Blank File in the Text Editor.

STEP 2: In Word, select all (Ctrl+a), copy (Ctrl+c), and paste (Ctrl+v) into the text editor.

What you will see is straight text. No paragraph styles and no italics or bolding or underlining. Tabs will be retained, so if you see suspicious indents, either a) manually delete them; or b) go back to the Word doc, remove the tabs and then copy/paste into a new text editor file.

STEP 3: Double-Check for Blank Lines.

In NotePad go to Format> Word Wrap and deselect it. (In other programs the word wrapping command might be found under Edit or View.) Each paragraph will become a single line of text. Scroll through the file to find any blank lines you might have missed. Remove them or tag them as deliberate blank lines.

STEP 4: Tidy the Italics.

You might notice, too, tags for italics are all over the place. (Word is very sloppy about applying italics.) In NotePad go to Edit> Find to open the search box and search for -STARTI-. Find Next will take you through the text file so you can neaten up the italics, deleting instances where blank spaces are italicized, and making certain tags are contained within paragraphs. This step is optional, but recommended.

Finish in Word

STEP 1: Open a blank doc in Word. This will be your Master Doc, edited, polished and prepped for formatting. Name the file accordingly.

STEP 2: In the text editor, select all (Ctrl+a) and copy (Ctrl+c). Paste (Ctrl+v) the text into the blank Master Doc.

STEP 3: Modify the Normal style.

In the Styles pane, hover the cursor over Normal and right click. Select "Modify".

Change the following:

> **Font:**
> Times New Roman
> 12pt
> **Paragraph:**
> Left align
> Indentation Special: First line By .25″
> Line Spacing: Single

Word should automatically update the Normal style. If for some reason it does not, select all the text (Ctrl+a) and apply Normal.

STEP 4: Modify all Heading Styles.
Style Heading (1, 2, 3, etc.):
> **Font:**
> Times New Roman
> 12pt (*no* bold or italic)
> **Paragraph:**
> Left align
> Indentation Special: (none)
> Line Spacing: Single

STEP 5: Apply Heading Styles.
If you did *not* tag Heading styles, use Find to search for the page or section break tags, set the cursor before each heading and apply the appropriate Heading style.
If you did tag Heading styles, use Find and Replace.

To apply Heading 1:

> In the **Find** field: -H1-*-ENDH1- and check "Use wildcards"
> In the **Replace** field: More> Format> Styles and select the Heading 1 style (leave the field blank)
> **Replace All**

To apply other Heading styles use the appropriate tags (-H2-, -H3-, etc.).

Delete the tags using Find and Replace.

> In the **Find** field: -H1- (make certain "Use wildcards" is unchecked)
> In the **Replace** field: (leave blank and click No Formatting)
> **Replace All**

Repeat this operation to delete the end tags and any additional Heading style tags.

STEP 6: Restore Italics and Other Special Formatting.
Use Find and Replace to restore italics:

> In the **Find** field: -STARTI-*-ENDI- and check "Use wildcards"
> In the **Replace** field: Format> Font> Italic (leave the field blank)
> **Replace All**

Delete the tags:

> In the **Find** field: -STARTI- (make certain "Use wildcards" is unchecked)
> In the **Replace** field: (leave blank and click No Formatting)
> **Replace All**

Repeat this operation for the end tag.

Restore bold and underlined text with the same method, using the appropriate tags in the Find field and formatting in the Replace field.

This styling flusters many writers. It creates an essentially unstyled doc lacking visual clues other than tags and notes to yourself. There is, however, a method behind the madness. The simplicity of the styles doesn't give Word opportunity to insert coding that requires the file to be cleaned again. The applied Heading styles create a navigation guide viewable in the Navigation pane, without inserting extraneous coding that requires additional clean up. You won't be reading this Master Doc (nor will anyone else) other than to make occasional updates if typos are discovered when proofreading formatted files.

From this Master Doc you can make as many copies as you need for as many purposes as you need—email, ebook, manuscript, print edition, etc.

In the chapters about formatting specific types of files, you'll see how this very simple, no-nonsense styling works to your advantage by reducing errors and increasing efficiency.

A bit of diligence on your part will ensure you always have an up-to-date version. Make sure to insert any changes to the text resulting from proof corrections or updates.

Be sure to update it, too, as you update digital storage systems. Keep your work archived, keep it safe.

To create a template for future Master Docs, do this:

1. Save As to make a copy and name it "Master Doc Template".
2. Modify the Normal and Heading styles by checking the box for "New documents based on this template".
3. Select all the text (Ctrl+a) and delete it.
4. Write reminders to yourself about using the Master Doc Template.
5. Save it and close.

The next time you need a Master Doc, open the template, Save As to make a copy, delete the reminder and the styling is set up and ready.

PART V

Formatting Word Docs for Specific Purposes

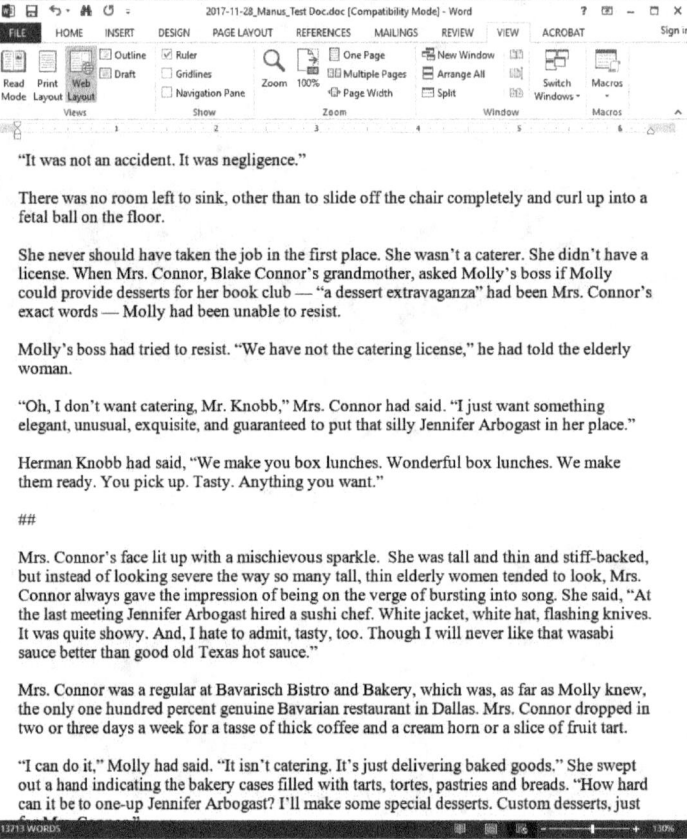

Text ready to copy and paste into the body of an email.

13: How to Format an Email

One question that I get quite often is this:

"Every time I copy/paste chapters of my novel into the body of an email it gets all messed up. Everything runs together! (Or there are significant font size changes, or everything is bolded, or there are broken lines, text runs off the screen, or, or, or . . . .) How do I fix this?"

Well, in the interests of science I have explored the situation and run experiments and have come to the conclusion it is not worth "fixing." There are countless email services and each one of them has their own style and set up and quirks. Trying to accommodate every one of them and forcing styling to work is an exercise in frustration. Life is too short.

The thing to remember is this: *Anyone who requests a synopsis or a few chapters in the body of an email is not in the least bit interested in style or formatting*. All they want is to read your words and make a decision. What follows makes it easier for you *and* the recipient.

STEP 1: Open a blank document.

STEP 2: From the Master Doc select the amount of text to embed in the email. Copy it (Ctrl+c) and paste it (Ctrl+v) into the blank doc.

STEP 3: Save and name the new doc.

STEP 4: Modify Normal.

> **Font:**
>> Times New Roman
>> 12pt
>
> **Paragraph:**
>> Align: Left
>> Indents: 0 (zero)
>> Special: none
>> Space Before and After: 0 (zero)
>> Line spacing: Single.

STEP 5: In Home> Paragraph activate the Show feature by clicking the ¶ icon.

STEP 6: Select all the text (Ctrl+a) and apply the Normal style.

What about Heading styles? Some email programs recognize Word's Heading styles and some do not. At this point it doesn't matter. Any agent or editor who requests material embedded in the body of an email—to prevent viruses and other malware in attachments—is used to reading material in an email and will recognize headings even without styling.

If styles other than Normal remain in the doc, select all the text, and in Home> Font click the "Clear all formatting" icon. (It looks like an A with an eraser.) Apply Normal to the text.

STEP 7: Double check that *all* deliberate blank lines and scene breaks are tagged. Double check that *all* comments to yourself have been addressed and delete the comments.

STEP 8: Insert blank lines between paragraphs using Find and Replace.

> In the **Find** field: ^p
> In the **Replace** field: ^p^p
> **Replace All**

STEP 9: Scroll through and delete any extra blank lines before and after deliberate blank line and scene break tags.

Now you have text with minimal styling, in a font that can be read by almost every program in existence, with blank lines between block paragraphs, that can easily be copy/pasted into the body of an email. It isn't pretty, but it is functional no matter what email programs you and the recipient are using.

To create a template for future email submissions, do this:

1. Save As to make a copy and name it "Email Template".
2. Modify the Normal style by checking the box for "New documents based on this template".
3. Select all the text (Ctrl+a) and delete it.
4. Write a reminder to yourself about using the Email Template.
5. Save and close.

The next time you need to make an email submission, open the template, Save As to make a copy, delete the reminder and the styling is set up and ready.

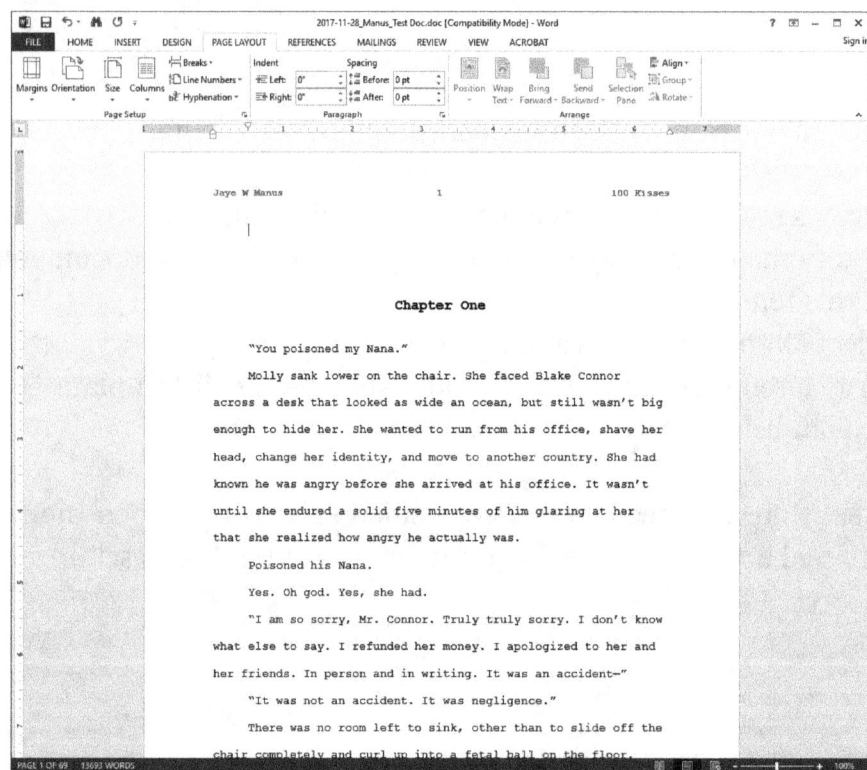

No-frills manuscript format.
Ready for editorial work, hard-copy submission or printing for archives.

14: How to Format a Manuscript

Some editors prefer a manuscript—a hard copy. Some writers prefer doing editorial chores on hard copy. Some writers want a safe, secure, non-digital copy of their work to wrap in sealed plastic and store safely away. What follows is a no-frills layout editors and posterity will thank you for.

STEP 1: Set up the Doc.
Open the Master Doc and Save As to make a copy. In View> Views select Print Layout. In Home> Paragraph click the ¶ icon to activate Show.

STEP 2: Set up the Page.
In Page Layout> Page Setup> Size select Paper Size 8.5" by 11".
In Page Layout> Page Setup> Margins select 1" margins all around.

STEP 3: Modify Normal and Heading Styles.
Normal:
Font:
Courier or Courier New*
12pt
Paragraph:
Align: Left
Paragraph Indent: 0.5"
Space Before and After: 0
Line Spacing: Double
Paragraph> Line and Page Breaks:
Check Widow/Orphan control

* Why Courier? It's the most common of the common fonts and contains a large subset of special characters. Utilitarian, not very pretty, but

comfortable to read in long form on either paper or on a screen. And, being a monofont, it makes calculating the page count for a print edition easier.

Heading 1:

Font:
    Courier or Courier New
    14pt (bold or italic optional)
Paragraph:
    Align: Center
    Paragraph Indent: none (zero)
    Space Before: 36pt
    Space After: 12pt
    Line Spacing: Double

Heading 2, 3, etc. if present in the doc:

Font:
    Courier or Courier New
    14pt (bold or italic optional)
Paragraph:
    Align: Left
    Paragraph Indent: none (zero)
    Space Before: 6pt
    Space After: 6pt
    Line Spacing: Double

STEP 4: Scene Breaks.

The scene breaks are tagged and any editor will recognize that ## on a line by itself indicates a scene break. For something fancier, try this:

Use Find to search for a scene break tag. Select the tag. Click the "New Style" icon at the bottom left of the Styles Pane. Name the new style Scene Break and base it on Normal.

Font:
  Courier or Courier New
  12pt
Paragraph:
  Align: Center
  Paragraph Indent: None (zero)
  Space Before: 3pt
  Space After: 3pt
  Line Spacing: Double

Use Find and Replace to change the tags.

In the **Find** field: ##
In the **Replace** field: *** and select Format> Style> Scene
Break
Replace All

STEP 5: Deliberate Blank Lines.

My preference is to leave in place tags for deliberate blank lines—it clears up any confusion in those cases where the line occurs at the top or bottom of a page. If you would prefer to delete them, use Find and Replace:

In the **Find** field: ^p#^p (If you invented your own tag, use it:
^pYOUR TAG^p)
In the **Replace** field: ^p^p
Replace All

STEP 6: Notes to Yourself and Special Formatting.

In the **Find** field: [
(If you used some other method or character to identify
character or styling tags, search for that.)

Address each note to yourself and delete it. Remember, this is not a "formatted" doc. There is no need for noting areas of special formatting. If you are printing it for your own purposes, the notes are mere clutter and can be deleted.

If you are submitting the manuscript to a publisher, they will make the design decisions. If using Replace All to delete the notes and plain text tags, be sure to check Match Case so that you do not accidentally delete actual text.

I do not recommend styling characters for variants such as superscript, subscript, small caps, all caps or smaller or larger sized words. Such styling is unnecessary for editorial purposes and can be distracting.

The one exception for styling is lists. Format those.

Select the entire block of text that comprises your list. In Home> Paragraph are three List style icons: bullet (unordered), numbered (ordered), multi-leveled (ordered). For quick styling of bulleted or numbered lists, click the desired icon and the selected text will be styled in the default list style. For multilevel lists, click on the List icon's down arrow to open the dropdown menu and select the style of list that suits your purposes.

STEP 7: Create a Header.
1. In Insert> Header & Footer> Header click the arrow for the dropdown menu.
2. Select Blank (Three Columns). A special HEADER & FOOTER toolbar will open.
3. In the left text field type your name.
4. In the center text field, insert the page number. Open the dropdown menu under Page Number and select Current Position, Plain Number.
5. In the right text field type the name of the book.
6. Close the Header by clicking the red icon in the toolbar or by double-clicking on the document text.

Word will automatically create a Header style that is based on Normal. It can be modified by hovering the cursor over the style and right clicking to open the Modify Style task menu.

The header spacing can be modified, too. Double-click on the header to open the Header & Footer special toolbar. In Position adjust the distance of the header text from the top of the page.

STEP 8: Page Breaks.
Use Find and Replace to create page breaks:

In the **Find** field: == (If you invented your own tag, insert that.)
In the **Replace** field: ^m^p
Replace All

STEP 9: Create a Title Page.

Doing battle with Word over page numbering is too much hassle. It's much easier to create the title page in a separate doc. Type your name, address, phone number and email address in the top right corner, center the book title and your name or pen name on the page.

Print.

STEP 10: Print the Document.

Go to File> Print and follow the menu for your home printer.

To create a template for future manuscripts, do this:

1. Save As to make a copy and name it "Manuscript Template".
2. Modify the Normal style by checking the box for "New documents based on this template".
3. Select all the text (Ctrl+a) and delete it.
4. Write a reminder to yourself about using the template.

The next time you need to create a manuscript, open the template, Save As to make a copy, delete the reminder and the styling is set up and ready.

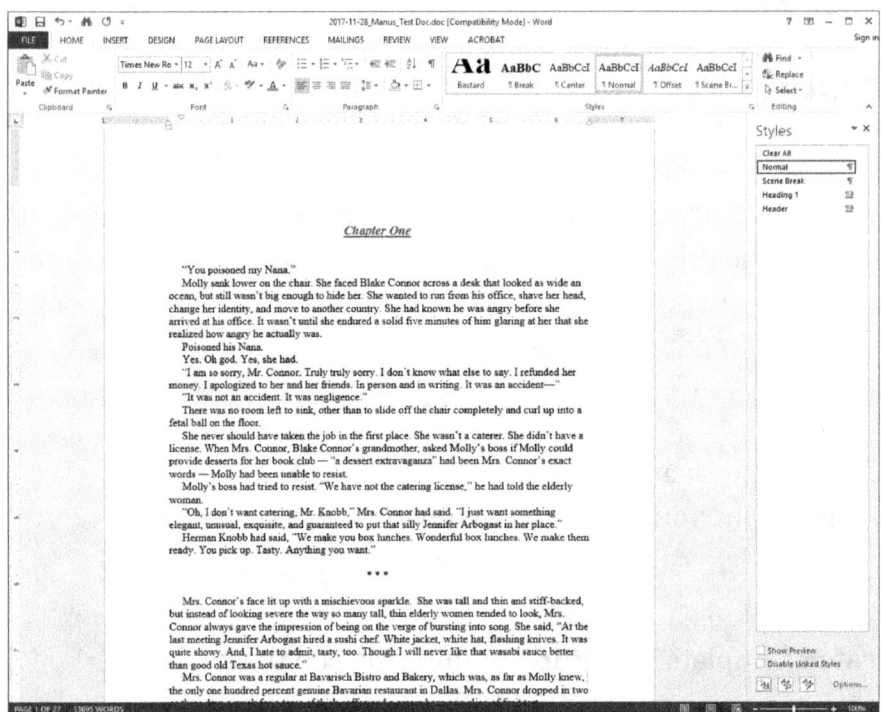

Doc ready for conversion as an ebook.

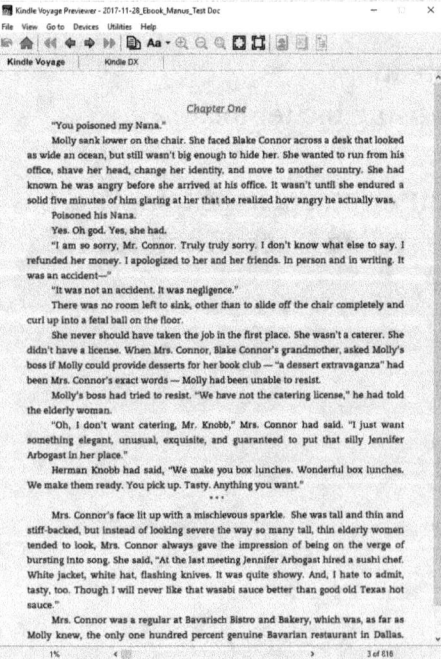

Ebook created with quickie conversion via the Kindle Previewer and ready for proofreading.

15: How to Format an Ebook

This reader's philosophy about ebooks:

A terrific story well told can make me forgive less than stellar ebook formatting. But *no* amount of superb design or fancy bits can make up for a bad story or a poorly edited story or a story that hasn't been proofread.

Make your *story* priority number one. Write, learn, rewrite (if you must), polish, and find help if you need it in the form of beta readers and/or editors. When the book is formatted, proofread it to root out any remaining typos or formatting goofs.

I *do not recommend* using Word to format a nonfiction ebook. Nonfiction is tricky enough using the proper tools to place images, create lists and multi-level tables of contents and so on.

(This caution especially applies to people who are actual Word pros, having taken the classes, having read the manuals, and are using Word in an office environment on a daily basis. Features that can create fabulous memos and reports can absolutely wreck an ebook.)

For formatting a nonfiction ebook I highly recommend:

a) Hire a professional formatter, or;

b) Learn basic HTML and CSS, or;

c) Use an epub editor such as Sigil, or;

d) Use an ebook creator program such as Jutoh or Vellum.

It is not difficult to format a novel or short story for an ebook in Word. In general the trickiest part is resisting the temptation to use the quick icons in the Home Ribbon. Many of the quick access tools can create problems in an ebook—including the icons in Font. (Bold, italic and underlining are safe. The rest are iffy.) Always use Paragraph styles *and* Character styles.

What follows will produce a problem-free ebook (novel or short story) that will convert seamlessly at any retailer or aggregator (such as Smashwords or Draft2Digital) that accepts a Word doc. It will render properly on whatever device readers are using, be it a computer screen, Kindle, iPad, Nook or smartphone.

Set Up the Doc

STEP 1: Open the Master Doc and Save As to create a copy.
Go to View> Views and select Web Layout.
In Home> Paragraph click the Show icon ¶.

STEP 2: Insert Front and Back Matter.

If you have not already included front and back matter for your novel or short story, create it now in a separate doc, scrub it clean, and copy/paste the text into the ebook doc wherever it needs to go. Insert the page break tag == when an entry requires its own "page".

A professional and perfectly acceptable layout for an ebook:

- Table of Contents (for a novel or novella—a single short story doesn't need one)
- Title Page
- Legal Information
- Dedication (optional)
- The Story
- Back matter (optional)
- About the Author with contact info (optional)

Note: What about the cover? Do **not** place the ebook cover in the Word doc. Doing so will cause your ebook to have two covers. When the listing is created, the conversion program at the retailer or aggregator will insert the cover into the ebook for you.

STEP 3: Modify Normal.

In Home> Styles open the Styles Pane by clicking the arrow in the lower right corner of the Styles box. Hover the cursor over the Normal style in the Styles pane and right click. Select Modify.

Font:
Times New Roman
12pt
Paragraph Indents and Spacing:
Alignment: Left
Indentation: Left and Right 0 (zero inches)
Special: First Line 0.2" *or* 0.25" (if you prefer a deeper indent)
Spacing Before and After: 0 (zero inches)
Line Spacing: Single
Paragraph Line and Page Breaks: Clear *all* boxes

Note: *Never* justify text in Word for an ebook format. Doing so can damage the ebook by locking margins and disabling user preference controls.

STEP 4: Modify Heading 1.

Hover the cursor over the Heading 1 style in the Styles pane and right click. Select Modify.

Font:
Times New Roman
14pt
bold (optional) and/or italic (optional)
Paragraph Indents and Spacing:
Alignment: Centered
Indentation Left and Right: 0 (zero)
Special: none
Spacing Before and After: 0 (zero)
Line spacing: Single
Paragraph Line and Page Breaks: Clear *all* boxes

Many devices do not recognize Word's Before and After spacing (top and bottom margins). It's better to use hard returns. A good rule for ebooks: Three hard returns in a row is the maximum.

Create a top margin for Heading 1 using Find and Replace:

> In the **Find** field: ^p==^p (If you used a tag of your own invention, use that instead: ^pYOUR TAG^p)
> In the **Replace** field: ^p==^p^p^p
> Use **Find Next** to insert the extra spaces where necessary.

Create a bottom margin for Heading 1. Click on a Heading 1 entry in the Navigation pane to take you to the beginning of a chapter. Place the cursor at the beginning of the first paragraph, and manually insert one or two hard returns. Do this for each chapter.

Front Matter

STEP 5: Table of Contents.
  Apply Heading 1 to the heading—call it either Table of Contents or Contents. The Normal style is sufficient for a list of chapters and sections.

STEP 6: Title Page.
  The title page is required by every retailer. It is informational and there's no need to make it fancy.

Title of the Book
Author Name

Select the title of your book. In the Styles pane, click on the icon for "New Style" (bottom left).

> Name: Title Page
> Style based on: (no style)
> **Font:**
> Times News Roman

14pt
bold (optional) and/or italic (optional)
Paragraph:
Paragraph Alignment: Centered
Paragraph Indentation Special: none

Insert two hard returns before the title and one between the title and author. Set the cursor at the beginning of each line of text and apply the Title Page style.

Some writers place the legal/copyright notice on the title page. Separate it from the author name using one hard return and style the notice in Normal.

Others opt for a separate page. Use a page break tag to separate the rest of the front matter from the title page. The Normal style is sufficient.

STEP 7: Legal Information/Copyright Notice.

Legal information isn't a legal requirement, as in there is no law saying an ebook has to contain a copyright notice, declaration of rights, disclaimer and publisher information. It is good practice to at least include the copyright notice:

MY STORY, copyright © 2017, by the Name of the Copyright Holder.
All Rights Reserved.

The notice won't protect you from pirates and plagiarists, but it does remove the "I thought it was in the public domain" excuse should you ever have to sue someone or issue a takedown notice.

PERMISSIONS: What *is* a legal requirement are permissions. If you have included excerpts from another writer's work or are using copyrighted poetry or song lyrics, *you must obtain permission and you must include those permissions in your ebook.*

DECLARATION OF RIGHTS (optional): There's no need to threaten readers with FBI prosecution and voodoo curses for the misappropriation of your work. It could offend honest readers and criminals will laugh at you. There is a suitable sample in Appendix A for you to use.

DISCLAIMER (optional): The "this is fiction and not based on real people" disclaimer offers you no legal protection whatsoever if someone can prove in a court of law that you have, indeed, based a character on a real entity in a defamatory manner. If you want to include a disclaimer (for the benefit of readers who have trouble separating fact from fiction) there is a sample in Appendix A for you to use.

PUBLICATION HISTORY (optional): If your novel or short story has been previously published include the publication history.

ISBN (optional): Every retailer assigns a unique identifier to ebooks, *but*, if your intent is to publish a lot of titles in print and have purchased ISBNs in bulk might as well assign numbers to the ebook edition. Each ebook platform type (MOBI, EPUB) is considered a unique edition and therefore requires its own ISBN. (If using Smashwords as an aggregator they will assign an ISBN for free or allow you to provide your own.)

PUBLISHER (optional): Writers create publishing companies for any number of reasons. Some formally register the company and obtain a tax ID for accounting purposes. Others envision a long career with many works and the publishing name creates an additional search term for readers to find their work. Still others want the possibility of publishing the work of other writers. *Don't* make the rookie mistake of including the line "Self-published by the author." Nobody cares and it makes you look like an amateur.

CREDITS (optional): Give credit where credit is due or, in the case of some stock photo licenses, where it is required.

Style the Story

STEP 8: Use Find and Replace to insert page breaks.

> In the **Find** field: ^p==^p (If you used a tag of your own invention, use that instead: ^pYOUR TAG^p)
> In the **Replace** field: ^p^m^p
> **Replace All**

STEP 9: Find the first scene break tag and select it. In the Styles pane, click on the icon for "New Style" (bottom left).

Name: Scene Break
Style based on: Normal
Modify:
Paragraph Alignment: Centered
Paragraph Indentation Special: none

Use Find and Replace to insert scene break indicators:

In the **Find** field: ## (If you used a tag of your own invention, use that instead: YOUR TAG)
In the **Replace** field: *** and select More> Format> Style> Scene Break
Replace All
Option: If you prefer an extra space above and below the scene break indicators, In the **Replace** field: ^p***^p
Option: If you prefer something other than asterisks to indicate a scene break, three bullet characters look nice. Do not use dingbat or ornament fonts—they will not render in the ebook. Be wary of special characters from the Symbols subset menus; you will have to test them to make sure they display the way you intend.

STEP 10: Special Paragraph Styles.

If your story requires special paragraph formatting, create new styles and make sure each is based on Normal. When creating a new style, select the first line or paragraph you want styled and then create the style. To apply it to other text, set the cursor at the beginning of the line or paragraph and click on the desired style.

POETRY AND SONGS

In the Styles pane, click on the icon for "New Style".

Name: Poetry Songs
Style based on: Normal
Modify:
Font: Italic
Paragraph Indentation Special: Hanging; By: 0.25″

NO-INDENT (block)

Because many conversion programs and many ereading devices *do not* recognize Word's top and bottom margin settings, it is important to separate no-indent/block paragraphs with a hard return.

In the Styles pane, click on the icon for "New Style".

Name: No Indent
Style based on: Normal
Modify:
Paragraph Indentation Special: (none)

OFFSET

An offset style is good for notes, letters, newspaper articles, etc. Because so many readers are using smartphones with small screens as ereading devices it's best to offset only the left margin.

In the Styles pane, click on the icon for "New Style".

Name: Offset
Style based on: Normal
Modify:
Paragraph Indentation Left: 0.25″
Paragraph Indentation Special: (none) *or* First line By: 0.2″ (if you prefer an indented paragraph)

CENTERED TEXT

Only use centered text for single lines of text. Centering full paragraphs, especially multiple paragraphs, looks weird and can be jarring for readers.

In the Styles pane, click on the icon for "New Style".

Name: Center
Style based on: Normal
Modify:
Paragraph Alignment: Centered
Paragraph Indentation Special: (none)

LISTS

In the case of lists it is okay to use the icons in Home> Paragraph. There is no need to create a List style. Keep it simple.

For a bullet list, select the text for the entire list. Click the arrow next to the bullet list icon and select the icon with the bullet. It is the only character that will render reliably in all ereading devices.

For an ordered list, select the text for the entire list. Click the arrow next to the numbered icon and select a numbering style.

Multi-level lists are not appropriate in ebooks.

⁊ ★ ʕ

After the special paragraphs are styled, do a search for the square bracket to ensure that all comments and tags are deleted.

SPECIAL CHARACTER STYLES

About using different fonts: it won't work. Conversion programs will ignore other fonts even if the fonts are embedded in a Word file. If your story requires multiple fonts you will have to use a program other than Word to format the ebook.

It's also important to *never* change font size for individual words *within* a paragraph. It can cause a conversion program to lock all fonts in the ebook and disable user preference controls.

That said, there are special Character Styles other than italics, bolding and underlining that will work in a Word format and will render in most ereading devices:

- Strikethrough
- Superscript
- Subscript
- Small caps
- All caps

Superscript and subscript text are very difficult to see in an ebook and can make line spacing wonky; use them sparingly.

All caps can overwhelm a screen, appearing to be oversized and mucking up already sketchy line spacing. Use sparingly.

Create Character Styles much the same as creating new Paragraph Styles.

Select text you would like styled. Click the New Style icon in the bottom left of the Styles pane.

Name the character style appropriately.

> Style type: Character
> Style based on: Default Paragraph Font
> Format> Font select an option from the Effects menu.

FOOTNOTES AND ENDNOTES

Never, *EVER* use Word's auto-footnote or auto-endnote features in an e-book.

If your novel or short story uses footnotes or endnotes, instead of using superscript single characters (number, asterisk, symbol) as designators do this:

[1] or [*] or (1) or (*)

It's not as elegant, but enclosing the designator in brackets gives you three or four characters to link and it's easier for readers to see on a screen.

Insert text for the footnotes at the ends of chapters and the endnotes at the end of the ebook.

An easy style for the footnotes/endnotes is to separate them from the story with ten underscores in a row and use the custom "Offset" style created for correspondence.

――――――――――

[1] This is the text for a footnote in Chapter 1.

Link footnotes and endnotes so readers can find the note quickly and then return to the text to continue reading.

To link the notes, first bookmark the designators:

1. Select the designator. Example: Let's call [1] the designator for the first footnote in Chapter 1.

2. Go to Insert> Links and click the Bookmark icon.
3. Type in a name for the bookmark (target for a link): chap1footnote1
4. The name can be anything as long as it begins with a letter, not a number, and has no spaces. An underscore is okay, but not a dash.
5. Click "Add".

Bookmark the footnote text by selecting its designator (in this Example the [1] that accompanies the text) and give it a name: chap1footnote1text

> Note: If it's helpful to view the bookmarks while you are working, go to File> Options> Advanced> Show Document Content and check the box for "Show bookmarks". Active bookmarks will look like highlighted text enclosed in brackets.

Link the footnote/endnote designators to the footnote/endnote text.

1. Select a designator to link: In this Example [1]
2. Go to Insert> Links and click the Hyperlink icon. Or use the shortcut Ctrl+k.
3. The selected text will appear in the field for "Text to display".
4. Click the icon for "Place in This Document".
5. In "Select a place in this document" scroll past Word's bookmarks to the end of the list to "Bookmarks" and click the bookmark where you want the link to go: chap1footnote1text
6. Click OK.

Ctrl+mouse click on the link you just created and it will take you to the footnote.

Select the footnote's designator and link it back to the story text.

STEP 11: Use Find and Replace to delete the deliberate blank line tags.

> In the **Find** field: ^p#^p (If you used a tag of your own invention, use that instead: ^pYOUR TAG^p)
> In the **Replace** field: ^p^p
> **Replace All**

STEP 12: Link Chapters to the Table of Contents.

While a table of contents for fiction is optional in print (and rarely used) it is essential in ebooks. While most ereading devices have a Go To feature for easy navigation, some do not. A publisher-generated table of contents is required by most online retailers and aggregators.

Because Word is bookmarking and linking Heading entries for the navigation guide, it makes sense to think that using Word's ability to auto-generate a table of contents would make this a one-step process. Especially given that conversion at online retailers and aggregators will use Heading entries to create internal navigation guides. Unfortunately, that does not work for publisher-generated tables of contents. You must manually create bookmarks and links in order to have a functional table of contents.

> Note: If it's helpful to see the bookmarks while you are working, go to File> Options> Advanced> Show Document Content and click the box for "Show bookmarks". Active bookmarks will look like highlighted text enclosed in brackets.

Bookmark the table of contents:
1. Select the heading for the Table of Contents.
2. Go to Insert> Links and click the Bookmark icon.
3. Type in a name for the bookmark (target for a link): ToC
4. Click "Add".

Bookmark the first Heading 1 entry:
Example: Chapter 1

1. Select the heading for Chapter 1.
2. Go to Insert> Links and click the Bookmark icon.
3. Type in a name for the bookmark. (The name can consist of letters and numbers, but must begin with a letter. No spaces allowed, but underscores are okay. Example: chap1 or chapter1 or chapter_1 are all acceptable.)
4. Click "Add".

To link the chapter heading to the table of contents, select the bookmarked text.

1. Go to Insert> Links and click the Hyperlink icon. Or use the shortcut Ctrl+k.
2. The selected text will appear in the field for "Text to display".
3. Click the icon for "Place in This Document".
4. In the box "Select a place in this document" scroll past Word's bookmarks to the end of the list to "Bookmarks" and click the bookmark you created: ToC
5. Click OK.

Hold down the Ctrl key and mouse click the link. It will take you to the table of contents.

Link to the chapter from the table of contents:

1. Select the text for the Chapter 1 entry in the table of contents.
2. Go to Insert> Links and click the Hyperlink icon. Or use the shortcut Ctrl+k.
3. The selected text will appear in the field for "Text to display".
4. Click the icon for "Place in This Document".
5. In the box "Select a place in this document" scroll past Word's bookmarks to the end of the list to "Bookmarks" and click the bookmark for Chapter 1.
6. Click OK.
7. Hold the Ctrl key and mouse click the link. It will take you to Chapter 1.

Repeat this process for every chapter in the book. It's optional to link to the back matter sections such as acknowledgements, the author bio, and a list of other works.

STEP 13: Back Matter.

Should you use the actual words "The End" for your novel or short story? It's silly in a print edition (unless you're being ironic), but it's actually helpful in an ebook since ebook readers don't have the same visual clues as print readers.

Adding "The End" clears up any confusion as to whether there is missing text or that the story is indeed over.

Back matter is optional. The ebook can end at "The End" and be perfectly acceptable. It is acceptable to include Acknowledgements, Notes from the Author, Notes from the Editor, Glossaries, Bibliographies, other references, Other Works by the Author, and About the Author.

An About the Author entry is optional, but *highly* recommended. Readers like it. Fans of your writing really, *really* like it if you include contact information so they can visit your blog, receive your newsletter, follow you on social media or even email you.

> Caution: Some readers (and retailers) consider excessive back matter to be deceptive, to trick readers into believing they are getting more story for the price or to game subscription programs by padding the page count. Reader complaints and nasty-grams from retailers are no fun, and having your account suspended can ruin your writing career.

In general, style back matter in Normal and give each section a heading with the Heading 1 style applied. That way entries will be included in the ereading device navigation guide (the Go To feature). To list back matter entries in the table of contents, bookmark and link the Heading 1 entries.

For such things as glossaries, bibliographies, and any other entries that appear as lists a simple style is to apply a "No Indent" style and insert a blank line between each entry.

LISTING OTHER WORKS

Should you list your other works? Of course. If a reader likes one of your books they may very well go on a hunt for something else written by you. (Bless the binge readers, am I right?) Listing other works is also highly useful for series. (Self-publishers take note: *Numbering* series titles is *extremely* helpful to readers.) For those writers who use multiple pen names, listing other works can lead to new readers who might not be aware that you write in different genres. Be smart about it, though. If you write stories for children under one name and erotica under another, it's wisest to keep those as widely separated as possible.

Where to place a list of other works?

Some writers prefer it in the front matter because it looks more traditional that way. Others want a list where readers will see it while they are excited from having read a good story and are hungry for more, so it's placed in the back matter.

Should you link your other works to the places where readers can buy them? Sometimes.

Every online retailer has a terms of service policy for users (ToS). Make sure you read it before setting up a publisher account. In general, if you are listing on a particular site, links to books being sold on that site are okay. Links to other retail sites are *not* okay, and that includes your own website if you happen to be selling books direct to consumers. For instance, any link to Amazon (including to Author Central) will cause your ebook to be rejected by Apple iBooks.

My recommendation is this: When the doc is styled, proofread and ready to go *except* for the links to your other books, do a Save As to create a copy for each online retailer or distributor with which you will set up an account. Tailor links to those websites.

STEP 14: Links to the Internet.

What to link? If you're the sociable type, link to Twitter, Facebook, Instagram or other sites where you have an active presence. Link to your website or blog. If you send out a newsletter, invite readers to sign up by including a link.* If it's okay for readers to email you directly, include your email address.

> * Invites with calls to action such as "leave a review and get a free book" can violate the terms of service at some retailers. Any time you ask the readers to do something in exchange for something, double-check the terms of service to make sure you are in compliance.

1. To create a link select the text you want linked.
2. Go to Insert> Links and click the Hyperlink icon or use the shortcut Ctrl+k.
3. The selected text will appear in the "Text to display" field.
4. In the "Link to" menu click "Existing File or Web Page".
5. In the "Address" field insert the *complete* url of the place you want the link to go.

6. Example: https://www.MYWEBSITE.com
7. To reduce errors, visit the site on the Internet and copy the url. Paste it into the Address field. Make sure there are no extra spaces before or after the url.
8. Click OK.

To link an email address go to Insert> Links and click the Hyperlink icon or use the shortcut Ctrl+k.

1. In the "Link to" menu click "E-mail Address".
2. In the "Text to display" field type the text you want readers to see: Example: Email me at author@mailservice.com
3. In the "E-mail address" field type in the email address. Word will automatically insert the "mailto" information necessary to create the link.
4. Click OK.

STEP 15: Converting the Ebook

If a site accepts Word docs, then the doc doesn't need to be converted into an EPUB or MOBI file. The retail site or distribution service will do the converting.

But . . . stuff happens. Things go wrong. Good intentions make messes. Mistakes are made. While almost every online retailer or distributor offers an opportunity to preview the ebook before clicking the Publish button, the option is clunky at best and time consuming at worst. Because of time constraints, it's difficult to proofread using the retail site previewers.

Caution: There are sites that offer to convert your doc into an ebook—for a fee. AVOID THEM. There are also sites that offer to convert a doc for free, except that at the same time they are turning your Word doc into an EPUB file they are infecting your computer with viruses, Trojans and other nasty malware. I can't say it loudly enough: AVOID THEM!

To convert the Word file into an ebook first download some programs onto your computer:

- MobiPocket Creator
- Calibre (ebook management)
- Kindle Previewer (from Amazon)

There are links to find them in Appendix A.

All three of the programs are freeware and safe to use. None of them requires any technical skill on your part.

MOBIPOCKET CREATOR is practically obsolete and its ebook viewer isn't very good (actually, it's awful). Once upon a time Amazon required ebook creators to use it to convert their ebooks before creating a listing. Amazon evolved, but MobiPocket hasn't and the files it creates aren't up to the latest standards. But it is still a very handy program for quickie conversions for personal use.

CALIBRE is an ebook management program that is much beloved by writers and readers. It will accept a variety of file types and convert them into different types of ebook files. It contains an epub editor (and last time I looked it was pretty good) and tools for inserting covers and metadata. It will *not* convert Word docs.

Calibre's viewer is far superior (in my opinion) to any other program of its type and it can be customized for reading comfort. The problem with the program is this: it does *not* produce *commercial quality* MOBI files to sell on Amazon. MOBI files can be converted and viewed in the Calibre viewer, they can be side-loaded onto any Kindle device, but using that file in an Amazon listing creates an ebook with many of the user preference controls disabled. There are ways to fix this in Calibre using its epub editor, but it's difficult. *Do not use Calibre to convert Kindle ebooks for commercial purposes.*

The KINDLE PREVIEWER is offered directly from Amazon. It will *not* convert a Word doc.

What makes it so useful is that it emulates different types of Kindle devices. It emulates how an ebook will look like on an e-ink reader or on a tablet or on a smartphone. You can adjust font families and font sizing and line spacing. It's not a perfect rendering—there are too many devices and updates for devices and the Previewer is not always in perfect synch because it's impossible to cover everything—but it's close enough to give you an idea about how your ebook will look to readers.

The Previewer allows you to view your book in DX mode which emulates pre-Paperwhite Kindles. Those models are less sophisticated than new e-ink readers and tablets, making DX-mode perfect for checking special characters. If the Previewer cannot read a character, it will indicate that with a ? in a box or gibberish. Problematic characters that will not display in DX-mode may or may not render in newer Kindle devices and may or may not render in Kindle apps. It is best to find substitutes for them.

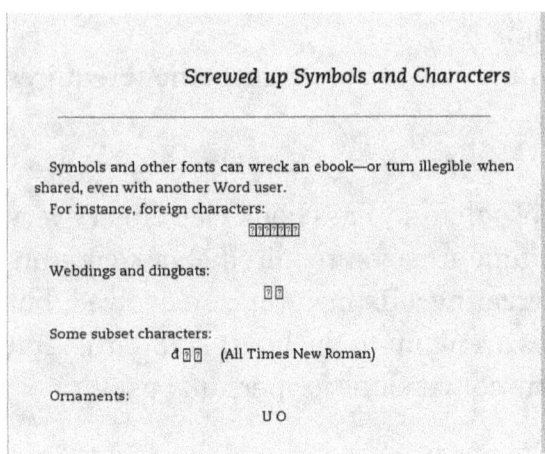

CONVERT THE WORD DOC

1. Save As the doc in the .doc format. Turn off Show/Hide by clicking the icon. Close the .doc file.
2. Import the Word doc into MobiPocket Creator and Build an ebook from it. This will create a folder on your computer containing several different files.
3. For viewing only, open the .prc file in the Kindle Previewer and it will create a file that can be viewed in the Previewer. (It will not create a .mobi file.) You'll be able to see how your book will look on different devices and with different settings. This is a good way to check special characters. Unfortunately, the conversion will *not* be complete for all types of devices. The styling will be uneven. You will *not* be able to check the internal navigation guide.
4. To create a .mobi file that can be side-loaded onto a Kindle device, open the .opf file in the Kindle Previewer. (The program will issue warnings, but ignore them.)

5. To create an .epub file, open the .prc file created by MobiPocket in Calibre and convert it to EPUB.

Once you have either an .epub or .mobi file side-load it onto a device (Kindle, Nook, iPad, smartphone, etc.) to proofread the text. Again, the styling may or may not be perfect, depending on the device. Proper conversion will happen when you upload the listing on a retail site.

With this quickie conversion, if viewing a MOBI file on a Kindle, you will not be able to check the internal navigation guide. That check will have to wait until you are creating the listing at a retail site. Calibre should display the internal navigation guide for the EPUB file.

> Note: It seems logical that you'd get a better ebook by first converting it and then using the resulting .epub or .mobi to upload to a retailer or distributor. Not true. Every conversion program inserts its own coding into the file in order to optimize it for the program. As you will see when using the Kindle Previewer or Calibre, results will be mixed. Additional coding by the ebook reader programs not only adds to file size, it can have adverse affects on the ebook once it's converted again (and every retailer *will* convert the ebook file, no matter what format it is, in order to optimize it for their own devices.) If you are using Word to format an ebook for a site that allows you to upload a Word doc, then upload the Word doc to the listing.

STEP 16: Proofread the Ebook.

The number one biggest mistake self-publishers make is to skip proofreading the ebook.

It doesn't matter that the book was edited and polished. Gremlins are going to sneak in. There might be goofs in the styling. Links get misdirected. It is much, much easier to find and fix errors now than it will be to update listings after the ebook is published.

The best way to proofread an ebook is to find someone else to do it. Copy blindness affects *all* writers. The brain is very helpful in "correcting" text so that you see what you *meant* to say rather than what is *actually there*.

If there is no one else, convert the Word doc using the above methods and load the ebook on a device. The different platform and view will help overcome copy blindness. If you don't have an ereading device, you probably have a smartphone. There are a multitude of free apps available for reading ebooks on smartphones.

If you don't have an ereading device or a smartphone, open the converted ebook in either Calibre or the Kindle Previewer.

If doing the proofreading yourself, make any changes or corrections directly in the ebook format Word doc.

If someone else is proofreading for you, provide a copy of the ebook format doc as a markup doc and instruct the proofreader to highlight every change and correction. (Do not use Track Changes.) That way you can easily see what they've done and accept or reject the change.

Make certain you also insert all changes and corrections into the Master Doc in order to keep it updated.

Use Find and Replace to delete highlights.

> In the **Find** field: Select More> Format> Highlight (leave the field blank)
> Go to Home> Font and open the Highlight dropdown menu. Select No Color.
> In the **Replace** field: More> Format> Highlight (leave the field blank)
> **Replace All**

STEP 17: Last Looks Before Publishing.

1. Run a search for all tags, comments and highlights to make certain they are all addressed and deleted.
2. Check that all links go to where they are supposed to go.
3. Make sure any changes to the text you made in the ebook doc are transferred to the Master Doc. (If you forgot to do this, make a new Master Doc. Do a Save As to create a copy of the ebook format. From the copy, remove any material specific to the ebook, go back to Chapter 12 and follow the steps to scrub clean the doc. This will be your new Master Doc.)

16: How to Format a Novel for Print on Demand

Because Word is an office productivity program and not a publishing program, formatting print-on-demand books can be a challenge. The view will be backward (mirror pages instead of facing pages); when an odd page break is inserted it won't display blank pages (but they will be there); and setting up headers and footers with book-type page numbering is touchy. The quality of print isn't as good as when using a publishing program such as Adobe InDesign or QuarkXpress.

That said, Word *is* capable of producing a POD novel that looks professional. A book designer can tell the difference between a novel created with Word and one created in a publishing program, but the average reader can't or won't care.

I *strongly* recommend obtaining the latest, most up-to-date version of Word. Yes, it is an added expense. (Though much, much cheaper than a subscription to Adobe Creative Cloud or purchasing a publishing program.) Early versions of Word lack the capability to export the type of PDF files required by print-on-demand services and many of the styling options are too crude for commercial print books.

The key to good book design is simplicity. You want your book to look better than a manuscript, but not be tarted up with extraneous ornaments and over-formatting. Your story is the star; let it shine.

For nonfiction, I don't recommend using Word to format the POD edition. It's possible, but chances are you will not be happy with the results. Either hire a professional or use a publishing program such as InDesign or QuarkXpress.

Before you begin formatting you will need to make some design decisions about the size of the finished book and which fonts to use.

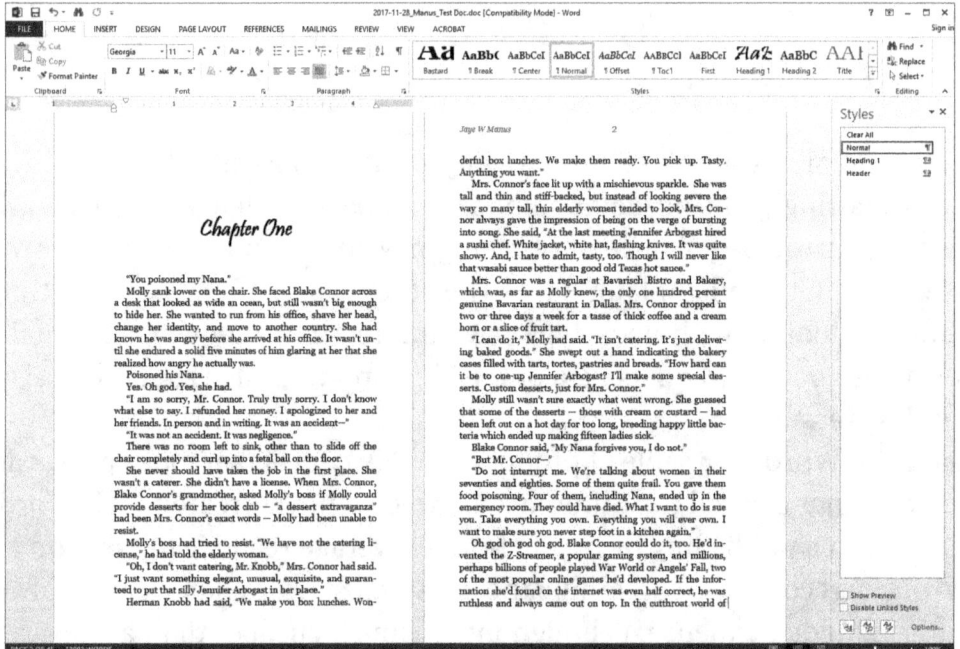

Print on Demand formatting.

Trim Size

Trim size is the overall dimension of the finished book. Print-on-demand companies offer standard and custom trim sizes. The best trim size for your book depends upon:

- Word count
- Number of chapters and sections
- Styling
- White space

It's best to keep the finished page count as low as possible without resorting to using very small fonts and super-tight line spacing. Print-on-demand technology is more akin to a high speed copy machine than it is to offset printing, and that means thicker paper. The higher the page count, the higher the cost of production and shipping, which means you will have to set a higher price on the book, and the higher the price, the less competitive it is in the marketplace. Reader comfort is also a factor. Over 350 pages, a POD book is unwieldy and over 450 pages it's downright uncomfortable to hold.

Guestimate the number of pages in a novel:

> 6″ by 9″ trim size: Divide the word count by 350.
> 5.5″ by 8.5″ trim size: Divide the word count by 300.
> 5″ by 8″ (or smaller) trim size: Divide the word count by 250.

With that formula, a 50k novel will be around:

> 6″ by 9″ trim size: 144 pages
> 5.5″ by 8.5″ trim size: 168 pages
> 5″ by 8″ trim size: 200 pages

Again, that's a rough estimate. The finished page count in any book will depend on the number of chapters, amount of front and back matter, fonts used, margins and white space.

Tip: Once you have decided on a trim size for the print edition, inform your cover designer and provide the back cover copy. The designer can finish the front and back covers while you are formatting the print edition. When you know the finished page count, the designer can finish the book cover spine.

Insert Front and Back Matter

A typical print novel contains in this order:

1. Title Page
2. Copyright Notice Page
3. Other Works by . . . Page (optional)
4. Acknowledgments (optional)
5. Dedication (optional)
6. Epigraph (optional)
7. Chapters
8. About the Author (optional)

If you are uncertain about what to include or the order in which it should go, go to your bookshelf or the library and look at novels in your genre. Use them as a guide. Traditional publishers, however, use a lot of legal language and publisher information that a self-publisher doesn't need; check Chapter 15: How to Format an Ebook for more details on what to include in the front matter.

Do a Save As of the Master Doc, name it "POD Text" and insert front and back matter. Be sure to insert break tags to separate the inserted pages.

Select Fonts

The pre-installed fonts in your computer used by Word are not optimal for a commercial print edition. More suitable fonts can be purchased. I've listed some sources in Appendix A. If you purchase a font for the body of the book, be certain to obtain the entire font family. For Headings and ornaments it's often possible to purchase a partial font. There are websites to find free fonts suitable for headings and ornaments.

If you envision a self-publishing career with many titles in the years to come, and you intend to do it yourself, a font is a good investment. (A really good font will cost around $250.00.) Once it's installed on your computer you can use it with any program. Most licenses allow using the font on up to five computers. Keep a backup copy in the cloud or on a portable storage device so it's on hand if you change computers.

If your budget does not allow for the purchase of fonts, the following list will give you decent results for body text fonts (most come pre-installed, depending upon which version of Windows or Mac OS you have):

- Baskerville
- Book Antiqua
- Bookman Old Style
- Garamond
- Georgia
- Palatino

Whether using a pre-installed font or considering a purchase, test the fonts before making a decision about which one to use. Most font foundries allow sampling before purchase. Create a mockup with paragraphs in different fonts. Use some italics and bolding, and be sure to include punctuation such as quote marks and various dashes. Export or Save As a PDF file. Print the PDF. This gives a fairly good (not perfect) emulation of what the font will look like in the actual book.

In a typical novel there are 11 to 14 words to a line and 28 to 36 lines per page. Some fonts are "spacey" and others are compact. Choose the font you think will be most attractive and comfortable for readers, and creates a page of text that falls within the normal range of words to the line and lines to the page.

It's acceptable to use one font family for the body text *and* the chapter and section headings, using italics, bolding and text effects for variations. It's also acceptable to use multiple fonts: one for the body text and another for the chapter and section headings. The biggest rookie mistake is to get carried away by using too many fonts. You want readers to get caught up in the story, not be overwhelmed by the book design.

Using a Template

For those new to do-it-yourself book designing, my number one recommendation is to use a template. It can save time and frustration by providing preloaded styles and font suggestions, plus taking care of the persnickety process of creating headers and footers and page numbers. Templates for print layouts are available at low to no cost. There are a few sources listed in Appendix A.

To use a template, download it and save it to your computer. Open the template in Word and do a Save As so the original is kept intact and in reserve in case you want to use it again. Or in case you have to start over.

Many templates contain instructions for their use. All require copy/pasting to "fill in the blanks."

If not using a template, follow the step by step instructions below.

Step by Step Format for POD

The order of the steps matters. As styles are modified and new styles are created and when text is hyphenated, the amount of text on any one page will shift. Following the steps in order will reduce the number of adjustments you'll have to make later.

STEP 1: Open the POD Text doc (contains front and back matter) and do a Save As. (Reserve the first POD Text doc in case you get tangled up and need to start over.)

STEP 2: Page View.
   In View> Views select Print Layout.
   Activate Show/Hide by clicking the ¶ icon in Home> Paragraph.
   Click Find to open the Navigation panel.
   Click the open arrow for the Styles pane. In Styles pane Options, "Select the styles to show", check "In use".

STEP 3: Page Size.

> Go to Page Layout> Page Setup> Size.
> Select "Custom size".
> For Width and Height use the trim size dimensions.
> Apply to: Whole document.
> Click OK.

STEP 4: Set Margins.

The margins in this example are suggestions. Your margins might need to be wider or narrower depending on the page count, trim size and design. *Do not* go less than 0.5" for the top, bottom and outside margins. The inside margin must be deep enough to keep text from running into the spine or forcing readers to crack the spine in order to read the book.

> Go to Page Layout> Page Setup> Margins.
> Pages: Mirror margins
> Top: 1"
> Bottom: 0.5"
> Inside: .85"
> Outside: 0.5"
> Gutter: 0"
> Apply to: Whole Document
> Click OK.

STEP 5: Set Layout.

> Go to Page Layout> Page Setup> Margins> Layout.
> Section Start: New Page
> Headers and Footers:
> Check "Different odd and even"
> Check "Different first page"
> From edge: Header and Footer: 0.5" recommended (*never* less than 0.25")
> Vertical alignment: Top
> Apply to: Whole document
> Click OK.

STEP 6: Modify Normal

Hover the cursor over Normal in the Styles pane and right click. Select Modify.

If you want this to be a template for future projects, check the box for "New documents based on this template" in the main task menu.

Font: (select desired font)
    Font size: for "spacey" fonts, 11pt; for "compact" fonts, 12pt
Paragraph:
    Alignment: Justified
    Outline Level: Body Text
    Indentation: Left, Right: 0
    Special: First line By 0.2"
    Spacing Before and After: 0
    Line Spacing: At least; At (for an 11pt font, 14pt; for a 12pt font, 15pt)
Line and Page Breaks:
    Check Widow/Orphan Control
Click OK.

STEP 7: Modify Heading 1.

Set the cursor at the beginning of a Heading 1 entry. Hover the cursor over Heading 1 in the Styles pane and right click. Select Modify.

If you want this to be a template for future projects, check the box for "New documents based on this template" in the main task menu.

Font:
    Choose desired font, font size and whether you want it bold, italic, underlined, or with special effects such as small caps, all caps, etc.
Paragraph
    Alignment: Left, Right or Centered
    Outline Level: Level 1
    Indentation: Left, Right: 0" for Centered alignment; your preference if the alignment is Right or Left
    Special: none
    Spacing Before and After: (6pt approximates one line of spacing. Determine where the chapter headings need to sit on the page and insert before and after spacing accordingly.)

Line Spacing: Match the spacing in the Normal style
Line and Page Breaks:
Formatting exceptions: "Don't hyphenate"
Click OK.

Modify any other Heading styles you might have used.

STEP 8: Ellipses
The ellipsis character looks clunky in print. In the majority of print books notice how ellipses are spaced: . . .

Spaced ellipses look better than the character and also aid in line spacing when text is justified.

To achieve the spaced effect modify the ellipses using non-breaking spaces to eliminate orphaned periods. It's a tad time consuming, but the effect is worthwhile.

Before spacing the ellipses, use Find and Replace to delete any spaces before or after ellipses throughout the doc.

In the **Find** field: Ctrl+Alt+(period)(space)
In the **Replace** field: Ctrl+Alt+(period)
Replace All

In the **Find** field: (space)Ctrl+Alt+(period)
In the **Replace** field: Ctrl+Alt+(period)
Replace All

In the Find and Replace fields I use (period) to indicate a period and (space) to indicate a blank space. The plus sign means hold all keys down at once.

Ellipses can be followed by punctuation such as question marks, commas, periods and quote marks. Use Find and Replace to change those first.

In the **Find** field: Ctrl+Alt+(period) (period)
In the **Replace** field: Ctrl+Shift+(space) (period)
Ctrl+Shift+(space) (period) Ctrl+Shift+(space) (period)
Ctrl+Shift+(space) (period)

What it should look like:

> **Find**: ....
> **Replace:** . . . .
> **Replace All**

With Show activated, the ellipses followed by a period looks something like this:

> text°.°.°.°. (The symbols are the non-breaking spaces.)

and without Show activated it looks like this:

> text . . . .

To Find and Replace ellipses with either commas or question marks or quote marks replace the final period in the Find and Replace fields with a comma or question mark or quote mark.

Some writers use an ellipsis at the beginning of dialogue:

> "...how can that be?"

To change those:

> In the **Find** field: "Ctrl+Alt+(period)
> In the **Replace** field: "(period) Ctrl+Shift+(space) (period)
> Ctrl+Shift+(space) (period) Ctrl+Shift+(space)
> **Replace All**

With Show activated, the results should look like this:

> ".°.°.°how can that be?"

For ellipses at the end of paragraphs:

> In the **Find** field: Ctrl+Alt+(period)^p
> In the **Replace** field: Ctrl+Shift+(space)(period)
> Ctrl+Shift+(space) (period) Ctrl+Shift+(space)(period)^p
> **Replace All**

For the remaining ellipses:

> In the **Find** field: Ctrl+Alt+(period)
> In the **Replace** field: Ctrl+Shift+(space) (period)
> Ctrl+Shift+(space) (period) Ctrl+Shift+(space) (period)(space)
> **Replace All**

STEP 9: Insert Section Breaks.

In order for headers, footers and page numbers to display properly, you must use section breaks rather than page breaks. Word disallows using Replace to insert section breaks, so this is a manual operation.

> In the **Find** field: == (or whatever page break tag you invented)
> Use **Find Next** to search for every place that requires a break.

Go to Page Layout> Page Setup> Breaks.

Place the cursor *before* each page break tag to insert the section break. This will cause the break to occur on the line above the tag, leaving a blank line (once the tag is deleted) to ensure a proper top margin in chapter and section headings.

I recommend leaving break tags intact until the final steps. They are a handy search term.

There are several selections in the dropdown menu for Section Breaks: "Next page"; "Continuous"; "Even page"; "Odd page". For a novel, these are the section breaks to use:

1. Title Page
2. "Next page": Copyright page
3. "Odd page": Other Works
4. "Odd page": Dedication
5. "Odd page": Epigraph
6. "Odd page": Chapter 1, page 1 (or Prologue or however the body of the novel starts)
7. "Next page": Chapters 2, 3, 4 etc.
8. "Odd page": First page of the back matter; all other sections in the back matter "Next page"

If your book has additional front matter such as an introduction, review blurbs, acknowledgements, etc., you will have to decide whether you want them to start on odd or even pages.

If, for some reason, your book requires a table of contents, go to Insert> Pages and insert the one or two pages the ToC will require and leave them blank except for a note to yourself: [TABLE OF CONTENTS HERE]

Note: Word will not display the blank page that occurs when the "Odd page" section break creates a blank page—the blank page *will* print. Check the page number at the bottom bar of the window and you'll see an odd number even while your eyes tell you otherwise. If this drives you nuts and you *must* be able to see the blank page, use a "Next page" section break (not a page break) and manually insert blank pages—using one section break for each blank page—to make sure the desired section starts on an odd numbered page. I recommend typing a note to yourself: [DELIBERATE BLANK PAGE] This will give you a visual aid when it comes time to insert headers and footers. The note can be deleted later.

Note: Some novels have all chapters start on an odd page. If your novel has 15 or fewer chapters, that style won't have much affect on the finished book size. If the novel has more than 15 chapters, the style could significantly increase the finished book size and increase production costs, so it's not recommended.

If your novel consists of many (over 50) chapters, consider a continuous style without any breaks between chapters. This involves modifying Heading 1 so that the Before and After white space isn't excessive and the styling of the chapter headings is distinctive enough so the reader is never confused. The entire body of the novel will be one section.

STEP 10: Scene Breaks (Part 1)

Go to the first scene break and select the scene break tag. In the Styles Pane click on "New Style".

Determine how much white space is necessary for scene breaks: 1 line, 1½ lines, 2 lines.

> Base the new style on Normal.
> Modify Paragraph Indentation: 0
> Modify Paragraph Alignment: Centered
> To create white space modify Before and After.
> For 1 line: Before 0; After 0
> For 1½ lines: Before 1pt; After 1pt
> For 2 lines: Before 3pt; After 3pt

Use Find and Replace to apply the Scene Break style:

> In the **Find** field: ## (or the tag you invented for the scene breaks)
> In the **Replace** field: ## and go to More> Format> Styles and select the Scene Break style
> **Replace All**

Don't delete the tags. Wait until Step 19: Scene Breaks (Part 2) to insert ornaments or other indicators and to delete the tags.

STEP 11: Headers.

Creating headers can be a persnickety process. Before you begin, do a Save As and reserve your POD doc as a back up just in case things get tangled up and it's easier to start over.

A common style for fiction:

- No headers in the front matter.
- Author name on the even pages.
- Book title on the odd pages.
- No headers on the chapter start pages.
- No headers in the back matter.

Create the Header:

1. Go to the title page and set the cursor before the first line.
2. Go to Insert> Header & Footer and click Header. (The special Header & Footer Tools Ribbon will open)
3. Select style: Blank (One Column).
4. Clear Options: Different First Page; Different Odd & Even Pages.
5. Delete the insert text field.
6. Go to page 1 of the story and set the cursor in the Header field.
7. Select style: Blank (Three Columns).
8. Check Options: Different First Page; Different Odd & Even Pages; Show Document Text.
9. Deactivate Link to Previous.
10. Delete all three insert text fields.
11. Go to page 2 of the chapter (even page).
12. Set the cursor in the Header field.
13. Select style: Blank (Three Columns).
14. Check Options: Different First Page; Different Odd & Even Pages; Show Document Text.
15. Deactivate Link to Previous.
16. Type the author name into either the left, right or center text field and delete the unused text fields.
17. Go to page 3 of the chapter (odd page).
18. Set cursor in the Header.
19. Select style: Blank (Three Columns).
20. Check Options: Different First Page; Different Odd & Even Pages; Show Document Text.
21. Deactivate Link to Previous.
22. Type the book title into either the left, right or center field and delete unused text fields.
23. Style the header by modifying the Header style Word will create automatically. Books on your shelf or at the library will give you ideas about simple and attractive headers.
24. Go to the first page of the back matter and set the cursor in the Header.
25. Select style: Blank (One Column).
26. Clear Options: Different First Page; Different Odd & Even Pages.
27. Deactivate Link to Previous.
28. Delete the insert text field.

Close the header and the special tool bar by clicking the red Close icon or double clicking on the document text.

STEP 12: Page Numbers.

Page numbers can be placed in either the header or the footer, and the alignment can be either right, left or centered. Page numbers can be styled separately from the Header style by creating a Character style.

A typical style for numbering pages in a novel:

1. Title page: no page number
2. Front matter: no page numbers
3. Chapter 1 (or Prologue), page 1: no page number in the header *or* the page number is placed in a footer
4. Chapter 1, page 2: Page 2
5. Following chapters: Continuous page numbers
6. Back matter: no page numbers *or* the page number is placed in a footer

To insert page numbers in the header but *not* on the first page of chapter starts:

1. Double-click on the header to open it and the special Header & Footer toolbar.
2. Go to Chapter 1, page 2 (even page) and place the cursor in the column where you want the page number to display. (The template has three columns: right, left and center.)
3. Click the arrow next to Page Number and in the dropdown menu select "Current position".
4. When the style menu opens select "Plain number".
5. Click the arrow next to Page Number and in the dropdown menu select "Page Number Format".
6. Start at: 1 and click OK.
7. Go to Chapter 1, page 3 (odd page) and place the cursor where you want the page number to display.
8. Click the arrow next to Page Number and in the dropdown menu select "Current position".
9. When the style menu opens select "Plain number".

To insert page numbers in a footer for *all* pages including the start pages of chapters and the back matter, but *not* the front matter:

1. Set the cursor on the heading for Chapter 1.
2. Go to Insert> Footer and click the arrow for the dropdown menu. Select "Blank (Three Columns)".
3. In the special Headers & Footers toolbar check Options: Different First Page; Different Odd & Even Pages; Show Document Text.
4. Deactivate Link to Previous.
5. In the footer, delete all three text fields. Set the cursor in the center column.
6. Click the arrow next to Page Number and in the dropdown menu select "Current position".
7. When the style menu opens select "Plain number".
8. Click the arrow next to Page Number and in the dropdown menu select "Page Number Format".
9. Start at: 1 and click OK.
10. Go to Chapter 1, page 2 (even page) and place the cursor in the column where you want the page number to display. (left/outside or center)
11. Click the arrow next to Page Number and in the dropdown menu select "Current position".
12. When the style menu opens select "Plain number".
13. Go to Chapter 1, page 3 (odd page) and place the cursor in the column where you want the page number to display. (right/outside or center)
14. Click the arrow next to Page Number and in the dropdown menu select "Current position".
15. When the style menu opens select "Plain number".
16. Check the pages in the front matter. If there are text fields or page numbers in the footer, delete them.

Close the Footer by clicking the red Close icon or by double-clicking the document text.

STEP 13: Style the Front and Back Matter.

There are two ways to style the Title Page.

One: Manually style the book title and author name using the Home task menus for Font and Paragraph. Set it up any way that suits you.

Two: Create styles, one for the title and another for the author. Creating styles for two lines of text might seem like overkill, but if you plan to produce several books and would like them to look consistent, styles make it easy.

Create new styles by clicking the bottom left icon in the Styles pane: New Style. Name the style for the book title: "Book Title". (Word also has a built-in style called "Title" and you can modify that if you want to.) Name the style for the author name: "Author Name".

If you want to use the styles in other projects, be sure to check the box for "New documents based on this template" in the main task menu.

For the Copyright page, create a style based on (no style). Modify it so the font is either 9pt or 10pt, and center it (if there are only a few lines) or use a block style (no paragraph indents). Use hard returns to drop the text to the lower part of the page.

Create styles for the dedication, epigraph, other works by . . . , and any other front matter that might be included. Use hard returns to align the top margins.

Do the same thing for the back matter, creating styles suitable for each section.

STEP 14: First Line Treatments

There are many ways to handle the first lines in chapters and scene breaks.

- Leave them as is
- No indents
- Extra deep indents
- Character styling such as the first three or four words in all caps or small caps or a different font
- Drop caps

My caution is this: Just because you *can* doesn't mean you *should*. Word offers a veritable cornucopia of text effects, but overusing them can create a mess that distracts readers and makes your book look amateurish. Use a light touch.

For a no-indent or deep indent style, create a new style based on Normal, name it "First Paragraph" and in Format> Paragraph modify only "Special indentation": (none); *or* give it enough of an indent to start the paragraph at approximately the middle of the line.

Go through the doc and apply it to appropriate paragraphs. (Use the break tag and scene break tag as search terms in Find.)

For a drop cap, set the cursor at the beginning of the paragraph where you want the drop cap, go to Insert> Text and click the arrow to open the drop cap task menu. Select a style and options.

To create a character style such as all caps, small caps or a different font, select "New Style" from the Styles pane. For "Style type" select "Character" and for "Style based on" select (no style). In Format> Font choose the font, font size, and special effects. Go through the doc, select the appropriate text, and apply the character style.

STEP 15: Special Formatting

Use Find to search for tags and notes to yourself for sections that require special formatting such as correspondence, headlines, poems, song lyrics, lists, etc.

Create styles to maintain consistency throughout the book.

A suggested style for correspondence:

> Based on Normal.
> **Modify:**
> Indentation: Left: 0.5"; Right: 0.5"
> Special: First line By 0.2"
> **Line and Page Breaks:**
> Formatting exceptions: Don't hyphenate

A suggested style for poetry or song lyrics:

> Based on Normal.
> **Modify:**
> Font: italic
> Alignment: Left

Indentation: Left: 0.5"; Right: 0.5"
Special: Hanging; By 0.25"
Line and Page Breaks:
Formatting exceptions: Don't hyphenate

After styling each instance of special formatting, delete its tag and any notes to yourself.

STEP 16: Images.
If your novel contains illustrations, photographs or graphics, use these specs:

- JPEG image (.jpg or .jpeg)
- 300 dpi (dots per inch)
- RGB color profile
- Images can be either color or black-and-white, but if you are printing in black-and-white, you will get better results if color images are converted to grayscale and adjusted so the darks are very dark and the highlights are bright enough so there is good contrast
- To prevent unsightly pixelation, the size of each image should be large enough so that it doesn't need to be enlarged in the print file. Scaling the image down to fit will not harm the quality
- If the images are larger than the width and/or height of the printed page, resize them to reduce the overall finished file size

Before you begin, place any images you intend to use in the same folder as your POD doc.

Use View> Zoom or the zoom scroll bar at the bottom of the screen to reduce the view to 75% so you can see the entire page. Or go to View> Zoom and select One Page.

To insert an image:

Place the cursor on the page where you want the image.

Go to Insert> Illustrations and click Pictures. An Insert Picture menu will open and you can search your computer for the image you want. Click on an image to highlight it and click Insert. (Do *not* copy/paste images into the doc.)

Double click on the image to open the special Picture Tools Ribbon.

ADJUST: Contains options for manipulating the image color and tone, plus has some filters for artistic effects. I recommend that before using these tools, you open another Word doc, insert an image and experiment with the features before deciding if you want to use them or not.

PICTURE STYLES: Contains options for borders, effects and layout. Again, open another Word doc, insert an image into it and experiment with the features to see if any are appropriate for your book.

ARRANGE: Contains options to set the image margins and for text wrapping.

SIZE: Options for cropping an image and for resizing an image. To resize an image, enter a number in *either* the vertical *or* horizontal size field. It will automatically resize the image to scale.

To place the image, size it first and then use the tools in the Arrange task menu to set it by itself or wrap it in text. The image can be manually dragged around to place it exactly where it should go.

To create Captions:

1. Double click the image to select it.
2. Go to References> Captions and click Insert Caption.
3. A task menu will open. Check the box: "Exclude label from caption".
4. Position: Below selected item
5. In the Caption field will be a number or letter that you can't delete. Type in the image caption anyway. Click OK.
6. The caption will be in a text box under the image.
7. Create a new Paragraph style using a font and font size appropriate for the design of your book. (Font size for a caption should be 2 or 3 pts smaller than the body text.) In Format> Paragraph set Special Indentation to (none) Select how you want the text aligned: left, centered or right.
8. Select the caption text and apply the Caption style. Delete the number or letter designator that Word inserted by selecting it and hitting the delete key until Word is convinced you really want it gone.

STEP 17: Footnotes and Endnotes.

If you followed recommendations in Chapter 5: "Formatting" on the Fly then the footnote and endnote text is in a separate doc. Open it now.

To insert a footnote:
1. Set the cursor where you want the footnote indicator to appear.
2. Go to References> Footnotes and click Insert Footnote.
3. A box will open on the page. Copy and paste the footnote text into the box.
4. To change the appearance of the footnote or change the numbering system or symbols used, click the arrow in the bottom right corner of the Footnotes box to open a task menu.

To insert an endnote:
1. Set the cursor where you want the endnote indicator to appear.
2. Go to References> Footnotes and click Insert Endnote.
3. A box will open on the page. Copy and paste the endnote text into the box.
4. To change the appearance of the endnote, or change the numbering system or symbols used, or determine whether the endnote is placed at the end of the document or at the end of a section, click the arrow in the bottom right corner of the Footnotes box to open a task menu.

STEP 18: Hyphenation

For any style you *don't* want hyphenated, modify the style. Go to Format> Paragraph> Line and Page Breaks. In "Formatting exceptions" check the box for "Don't hyphenate".

Go to Page Layout> Page Setup> Hyphenation. The dropdown menu options are "None", "Automatic" and "Manual".

"Hyphenation options..." opens a task menu with some limited options for setting parameters.

Clicking Automatic will automatically insert hyphenation throughout the document. Because Word uses an algorithm based on the same dictionary it uses for spell check, you may not always agree with its choices. (Mine insists "alt-hough" is acceptable. Um, no, no it is not.)

Clicking Manual will start an operation that takes you through the entire document paragraph by paragraph, giving you options to accept, adjust or reject hyphenation choices. I recommend using Manual hyphenation. It's tedious, but you have control—especially in regards to proper nouns and invented words.

STEP 19: Scene Breaks (Part 2)

A common style for scene breaks is to use white space except when the break occurs at the top or bottom of a page. For the top of the page or bottom of the page breaks, use a scene break indicator—three widely spaced asterisks.

Use Find to search for ## and when a scene break occurs at the top or bottom of a page, replace the tag with three widely spaced asterisks.

Delete all remaining scene break tags with Find and Replace:

> In the **Find** field: ##
> In the **Replace** field: (leave blank)
> **Replace All**

To insert ornaments, you will need to first install an ornamental dingbat font. (Window's Webdings and Wingding fonts scream "I made this at home!" and most aren't suitable for a commercial book. I've listed some sites in Appendix A to find dingbat fonts for little to no cost.) Or, if you purchased a high quality font, go to Insert> Symbols> Symbol> More Symbols and in "Font" select the font and then see if its subsets contain ornaments. Many do and many of them are suitable for a novel.

Modify the Scene Break style by changing the font to the desired ornament font.

Find the first scene break.

Go to Insert> Symbols> Symbol> More Symbols and in "Font" select the font that contains the desired ornament.

Select the scene break tag and replace it by inserting an ornament.

Use Find and Replace:

> In the **Find** field: ##
> In the **Replace** field: Copy the ornament and paste it into the Replace field (it will display as a Latin letter or symbol). Go to More> Format> Font and select the dingbat font that contains your ornament. Go to More> Format> Style and select the Scene Break style.
> **Replace All**

STEP 20: Table of Contents.

It's unusual for the print edition of a novel to have a table of contents. The exceptions are children's chapter books and those instances where an adult novel has chapter titles. (Even then, in the case of adult novels, few readers will miss it if it's not there.) Anthologies and short story collections should have a table of contents.

To automatically generate a table of contents go to References> Table of Contents. Place the cursor in the section of the front matter where you want the table of contents. Click on the arrow under the Table of Contents icon to open the dropdown menu. There are choices for built-in templates and for creating a custom table of contents.

Word will create a list of styles for the entries (TOC 1, TOC 2, etc.). Modify those styles to suit your book.

STEP 21: Last Looks.

Use Find to search for any tags or notes to yourself you might have missed. Delete the tags and notes.

Scroll through the doc and look for orphaned quote marks and orphaned dashes. Those two occurrences are unfortunate quirks of Word.

If you find one, place the cursor between the text and the quote mark or the dash. Go to Insert> Symbol> Special Characters. In the list is a character called "No-Width Non Break". Click Insert. With the Show feature activated it will look like a rectangle inserted between the letter and the punctuation. With the Show feature off it will appear as if nothing is there. This will prevent quote marks and dashes from being orphaned.

Maximize the Word window.

Go to View> Zoom and select Multiple Pages. This will give you a side by side view of the pages. Unfortunately, Word places the first page on the left even though it should be a right side page because it is an odd number (page 1). So, the pages will appear opposite of what will be printed in the book with the inside and outside margins reversed. It takes a little bit of getting used to.

Even so, it's a good way to scroll through the doc to see how the pages look together. Make sure your scene breaks and other white spaces are to your satisfaction. If you spot a problem in spacing, make adjustments.

The best way to make spacing adjustments within a paragraph or sentence is to select the troublesome sentence or paragraph. Go to Home> Font and click the arrow in the box to open the task menu and click Advanced. With that menu you can scale the characters, either condensing or expanding them, which will change the spacing on a line or in an entire paragraph.

Exporting as a PDF

Online printers require that an interior file be submitted as a PDF file and that it be ISO compliant. The color profile is PDF/X-1a:2001.

1. Go to File> Options> Save "Preserve fidelity when sharing this document".
2. Check "Embed fonts in the file" and "Embed only the characters used in this document".
3. Go to File> Options> Display "Printing options".
4. Check "Print drawings created in Word"; "Print background colors and images"; "Update fields before printing"; and "Update linked data before printing".
5. Save As and select file type PDF.
6. When the save task menu opens, check the box "Open file after publishing".
7. Select Options.
8. Check the box for "All".
9. Check the box for "Document".
10. Clear all the boxes under "Include non-printing options".
11. In "PDF options" check the box for "ISO 1900S compliant".
12. Click OK.
13. Save.

The PDF file will open automatically in a pdf reader. Zoom out until the pages look about book size and scroll through, checking that everything is in place and the page numbering is correct.

Let your cover designer know the final page count so the book cover spine can be finalized.

ꙮ ★ ❧

If your PDF file is rejected by a print-on-demand service it will most likely be for one of two reasons: 1) the images are not 300dpi; or 2) the color profile in the PDF is incorrect (not PDF/X-1a:2001).

If the problem is the images, you will have to resize them in a photo or graphics program (such as Photoshop or Paint.net) so that they are 300dpi, then delete the images in the doc and replace them with the resized images.

If the problem is the color profile, the PDF will have to be converted. There are some online services that will convert the file (the Word doc or the PDF) for a low cost.

It is also easy to do with Adobe Acrobat. If you do not have Adobe Acrobat, send an email to jayewmanus@gmail.com and put "I read your book—help!" in the subject line.

Attach your PDF file.

If I'm at the computer when the email arrives, I can convert your PDF in about 15 seconds and send you the new PDF by return email. If I'm not at the computer it might take a little longer to get to it, but it won't take long.

Proofreading the Print-on-Demand Book

The best way to proofread the POD book is to create the listing at the printing service and order two proof copies: one for you and another to be sent to a proofreader.

If doing it yourself, when it comes in the mail, grab a red pencil or highlighter, settle into a comfy chair and go through the book. The proof copy not only allows you to check the text for typos and format goofs, but gives you a chance to examine the cover, too.

Another way is to print a copy. Depending on your printer and the size of the book, this can be slow and expensive. If you do not have a printer or you have one but it's very slow or it gulps toner the way some people eat M&Ms, many office supply stores and copy shops will print the PDF on a high speed laser printer.

The least expensive way is to proofread the PDF on your computer or tablet. (This can be very hard on the eyes, so take frequent rests away from the screen and don't forget to blink.) If your PDF reader allows highlighting and commenting directly on the PDF, do so. When finished, manually insert the changes and corrections into the Word doc.

Make sure any corrections to the text are inserted into the Master Doc so you have an up-to-date version.

Appendix A
Useful Hotkeys

When using hotkeys, + means press all the keys at the same time.

To select all the text in a doc: Ctrl+a
To copy selected text: Ctrl+c
To paste selected text: Ctrl+v
To cut selected text: Ctrl+x (unlike deleted text, cut text can be pasted elsewhere)
To undo: Ctrl+z
To save: Ctrl+s
To apply styles: Ctr+Shift+s (this opens a quickie menu box)
To open the hyperlink task menu: Ctrl+k

Useful Shortcuts

em dash: Ctrl+Alt+- (minus sign on the number keypad)
en dash: Ctrl+- (minus sign on the number keypad)
ellipsis: Ctrl+Alt+. (period)
Optional hyphen: Ctrl+- (dash on the keyboard)
Copyright symbol ©: Alt+Ctrl+c
Registered mark ®: Alt+Ctrl+r
Trademark symbol ™: Alt+Ctrl+t

Useful Find and Replace Terms

Paragraph (hard return): ^p
Soft return (line feed): ^l (lower case L)
Page break: ^m
em dash: ^+
en dash: ^=
Optional hyphen: ^- (dash on keyboard)
Tab: ^t

All of the above can be used as either Find or Replace terms. More can be found in Find and Replace> More> Special. The following are used only in Find *or* Replace.

(Find) All Text: ^?
(Replace) All Text: ^& (Use when wrapping text in open and close tags)
(Find) Section break: ^b
(Find) All Characters: * (Use with wildcards)

Online Resources for Self-Publishers

Distributors that accept Word docs for ebooks
Smashwords (www.smashwords.com)
Draft2Digital (www.draft2digital.com)
Amazon Kindle Direct Publishing (kdp.amazon.com)
Barnes & Noble Nook Press (www.nookpress.com)

Programs Useful for Writers
Scrivner (www.literatureandlatte.com)
LibreOffice (www.libreoffice.org)
Scribus (www.scribus.net)
FocusWriter (gottcode.org/focuswriter)

Programs Useful for Self-Publishers
Dropbox (cloud storage) (www.dropbox.com)
Adobe Creative Cloud (contains Photoshop, Illustrator, InDesign, and a host of other programs) (www.adobe.com/creativecloud.html)
Adobe Acrobat Pro (pdf reader/editor) (acrobat.adobe.com)
Paint.net (www.getpaint.net)
Gimp (www.gimp.org)
Notepad++ (text editor) (notepad-plus-plus.org)
Kindle Previewer (www.amazon.com/gp/feature.html)
MobiPocket Creator (download.cnet.com/Mobipocket-Creator)
Calibre (calibre-ebook.com)
Fonts
dafont.com (free fonts)
fontsquirrel.com (free fonts)

fontspring.com
fontbros.com
MyFonts.com

Caution: There are more places to find fonts than I can count or list here. Many sites that offer free fonts for download are malicious in that they will infect your computer with viruses and adware and other nasties. Be very careful about using free sites. Also, when purchasing fonts read the licensing terms carefully.

EPUB Editors
Sigil (github.com/Sigil-Ebook/Sigil)
Jutoh (www.jutoh.com)
Vellum (Mac only) (vellum.pub)

Images
iStock.com
bigstock.com
dreamstime.com
Pixabay.com
Freepik.com
shutterstock.com
30 free public domain image websites (use with care) (99designs.com/blog/resources/public-domain-image-resources/Business)

Copyright, ISBN and Legal
Bowkers (ISBN) (bowkers.com)
www.uspto.gov/trademarks-getting-started/trademark-basics/trademark-patent-or-copyright
www.copyright.gov/registration
fairuse.stanford.edu/overview/introduction/getting-permission

Print on Demand Templates
www.bookdesigntemplates.com
www.createspace.com/pub/simplesitesearch.search.do?sitesearch_query=Templates&sitesearch_type=SITE

Websites for Editing and Proofreading

Alan Cooper's Homonym List (www.cooper.com/alan/homonym_list.
html)
www.merriam-webster.com
www.grammarbook.com
grammarguide.copydesk.org

Copyright Notice

Sample:

> All rights reserved. This book or parts thereof may not be reproduced in any form, stored in any retrieval system, or transmitted in any form by any means—spoken, written, photocopy, printed, electronic, mechanical, recording, or otherwise through any means not yet known or yet in use—without prior written permission of the publisher, except for purposes of review.

Disclaimer for Fiction

Sample:

> This is a work of fiction. The names, characters, places, and incidents are products of the writer's imagination or have been used fictitiously and are not to be construed as real. Any resemblance to persons, living or dead, actual events, locales or organizations is entirely coincidental.

Appendix B: Customize Word

Go to File> Options

AutoCorrect, Options → PROOFING
AutoFormat, Options → PROOFING
AutoRecover → SAVE
Background colors and images → DISPLAY
Backup Copy, Automatically create → ADVANCED: Save
Bookmarks, Show → ADVANCED: Show document content
Colors, Show background → ADVANCED: Show document content
Cursor, Options → ADVANCED: Editing Options
Documents, Access → ADVANCED: Display
Documents, Recent → ADVANCED: Display
Drawings, Print → DISPLAY
Font, Substitution → ADVANCED: Show document content
Fonts, Embed → SAVE
Grammar, Check as You Type → PROOFING
Horizontal Scroll Bar → ADVANCED: Display
Hyperlink, Ctrl+Click → ADVANCED: Editing Options
Image, Size → ADVANCED: Image Size and Quality
Layout, View → DISPLAY
Live Preview → GENERAL
Measurements, Options → ADVANCED: Display
Mini Toolbar → GENERAL
Page Options → DISPLAY
Paragraph Style, Default → ADVANCED: Editing Options
Pasting, Options → ADVANCED: Cut, copy and paste
Print, Options → ADVANCED: Print
Quick Access Toolbar, Customize → QUICK ACCESS TOOLBAR
Ribbon Toolbar, Customize → CUSTOMIZE RIBBON
Save, Background → ADVANCED: Save
Save, Options → SAVE
ScreenTip → GENERAL

Security → TRUST CENTER

Select, Options → ADVANCED: Editing Options

Shortcut Keys, Show Options → ADVANCED: Display

Shortcuts, Keyboard, Customize → CUSTOMIZE RIBBON

Sound, feedback → ADVANCED: General

Spacing, Soft Return (Shift+Enter) → ADVANCED: Layout options for:

Spelling, Check as You Type → PROOFING

Tool tips, Show on Hover → DISPLAY

Underline, Spaces → ADVANCED: Layout options for:

User Name, Personalize → GENERAL

Vertical Ruler → ADVANCED: Display

Vertical Scroll Bar → ADVANCED: Display

Appendix C: Where do I find . . . ?

Accept, Track Changes → REVIEW> Changes

Align, Center → HOME> Paragraph

Align, Justify → HOME> Paragraph

Align, Left → HOME> Paragraph; or → HOME> Paragraph open arrow for task menu

Align, Right → HOME> Paragraph

Alphabetize → HOME> Paragraph> Sort icon

AutoCorrect, Options → INSERT> Symbol dropdown menu> More Symbols

AutoFormat, Options → INSERT> Symbol dropdown menu> More Symbols> AutoCorrect

Blank Page, Insert → INSERT> Pages

Bold → HOME> Font

Bookmark → INSERT> Links

Borders → HOME> Paragraph dropdown menu

Break, Page → PAGE LAYOUT> Page Setup dropdown menu

Break, Section → PAGE LAYOUT> Page Setup dropdown menu

Captions → REFERENCES> Captions

Case, Change → HOME> Font dropdown menu

Clear Formatting → HOME> Font

Clipboard, Task Menu → HOME> Clipboard open arrow for task menu

Color, Font → HOME> Font dropdown menu

Columns → PAGE LAYOUT> Page Setup dropdown menu

Comment, Delete → REVIEW> Comments

Comment, Go to Next → REVIEW> Comments

Comment, Go to Previous → REVIEW> Comments

Comment, New → REVIEW> Comments

Comment → INSERT> Comments

Comments, Show → REVIEW> Comments

Cover Page, Template → INSERT> Pages dropdown menu

Definitions, Words → REVIEW> Proofing

Drop Cap → INSERT> Text dropdown menu

Endnotes, Insert → REFERENCES> Footnotes dropdown menu

Find and Replace Results → Navigation Pane

Find → HOME> Editing dropdown menu
Font, Color → HOME> Font dropdown menu
Font, Family → HOME> Font
Font, Size → HOME> Font
Font, Task Menu → HOME> Font open arrow
Footer → INSERT> Header & Footer dropdown menu
Footnotes, Go to Next → REFERENCES> Footnotes
Footnotes, Insert → REFERENCES> Footnotes
Footnotes, Task Menu → REFERENCES> Footnotes open arrow
Formatting, Clear → HOME> Font
Gridlines, Show → VIEW> Show
Header → INSERT> Header & Footer dropdown menu
Header & Footer Special Toolbar → Double-click on either the header
 or the footer.
Headings, Navigation → Navigation Pane
Highlighter → HOME> Font dropdown menu
Hyperlink → INSERT> Links
Hyphenation → PAGE LAYOUT> Page Setup dropdown menu
Images, Alignment → PAGE LAYOUT> Arrange
Images, Insert → INSERT> Illustrations
Indent, Decrease → HOME> Paragraph dropdown menu
Indent, Increase → HOME> Paragraph dropdown menu
Indent, Paragraph → PAGE LAYOUT> Paragraph
Italics → HOME> Font
Language → REVIEW> Language dropdown menu
List, Bullet → HOME> Paragraph dropdown menu
List, Multi-level → HOME> Paragraph dropdown menu
List, Number → HOME> Paragraph dropdown menu
Margins → PAGE LAYOUT> Page Setup dropdown menu
Markup → REVIEW> Tracking
Multiple Pages, Zoom → VIEW> Zoom
Navigation Pane → HOME> Editing click Find
Orientation, Paper → PAGE LAYOUT> Page Setup dropdown menu
Page Break → INSERT> Pages
Page Numbers → INSERT> Header & Footer dropdown menu
Page Width, Zoom → VIEW> Zoom
Pages, Navigation → Navigation Pane
Paragraph Spacing → DESIGN> Document Formatting dropdown menu

Paragraph, Task Menu → HOME> Paragraph open arrow

Paste, Options → HOME> Clipboard dropdown menu

Pictures Special Toolbar → Double-click on any picture inserted in doc

Print Layout, View → VIEW> Views

Reject, Track Changes → REVIEW> Changes

Replace → HOME> Editing

Ruler, Show → VIEW> Show

Select → HOME> Editing dropdown menu

Shading → HOME> Paragraph dropdown menu

Shortcut Keys, Create → INSERT> Symbol dropdown menu> More Symbols

Show/Hide → HOME> Paragraph

Size, Paper → PAGE LAYOUT> Page Setup dropdown menu

Spacing, Before and After → PAGE LAYOUT> Paragraph

Spacing, Line → HOME> Paragraph open arrow for task menu

Spacing, Paragraph → HOME> Paragraph open arrow for task menu

Special Characters → INSERT> Symbol dropdown menu

Spell Check → REVIEW> Proofing

Strikethrough → HOME> Font

Style, Modify → Hover over style, right click, select Modify

Style, New → Styles Pane, icon bottom left

Styles Pane, Options → STYLES PANE> Options...

Styles, Pane → HOME> Styles open arrow

Styles → HOME> Styles

Subscript → HOME> Font

Superscript → HOME> Font

Symbols → INSERT> Symbol dropdown menu

Table of Contents, Add Content → REFERENCES> Table of Contents dropdown menu

Table of Contents, Create → REFERENCES> Table of Contents dropdown menu

Table of Contents, Update → REFERENCEs> Table of Contents dropdown menu

Tables → INSERT> Tables dropdown menu

Text effects → HOME> Font open arrow for task menu

Thesaurus → REVIEW> Proofing

Track Changes, Task Menu → REVIEW> Tracking

Track Changes → REVIEW> Tracking

Translate Words → REVIEW> Language dropdown menu
Underline → HOME> Font dropdown menu
Web Layout, View → VIEW> Views
Word Count → REVIEW> Proofing
Zoom → VIEW> Zoom

Acknowledgements

First, I need to thank all the readers of my blog who have emailed questions about using Word which sent me scrambling in search of answers.

Second, very special thanks to Julia Rachel Barrett and Marina Bridges who allowed me, in the beginning, to muck around with their writing projects so I could learn how to format ebooks. (How hard can it be? Right, ladies?)

Third, most especially thank you to Lawrence Block. Restoring and producing his extensive backlist taught me far more about using a word processor than anyone outside a bureaucracy needs to know.

Fourth, a special thank you to Jerrold Mundis for a) pushing me to find answers to difficult questions; and for b) writing *Break Writer's Block Now!*

Fifth, a shout out to Bill Vaz, organizing guru and stern voice of reason. Thank you, little brother, couldn't have done this without you.

Jaye W Manus is a book producer—Lawrence Block calls her the "Goddess of Production and Design"—whose closet now contains many hats: Writer, Editor, Formatter, Proofreader, and Cover Designer. In 2011, with zero technical knowledge and an attitude of "Well, how hard can it be?" she began formatting ebooks which led to backlist restoration which led to formatting print-on-demand books which led to cover design. You can follow her journey on her blog, QA Productions, where she's been sharing what she's learned over the years and occasionally rants about various and sundry subjects.

www.ingramcontent.com/pod-product-compliance
Lightning Source LLC
Chambersburg PA
CBHW081559220526
45468CB00010B/2701